Gran's Bees

By Mary Thompson   **Illustrated by Donna Peterson**

The Millbrook Press
Brookfield, Connecticut

Library of Congress Cataloging-in-Publication Data
Thompson, Mary, 1947–
Gran's bees / by Mary Thompson; illustrated by Donna Peterson.
p.   cm.
Summary: On a visit to her grandmother's farm, Jessie discovers the secrets
of beekeeping that will allow her to carry on her grandmother's work.
ISBN 1-56294-652-8 (lib. bdg.)
[1. Bee culture—Fiction. 2. Bees—Fiction. 3. Grandmothers—
Fiction.] I. Peterson, Donna, 1968– ill. II. title.
PZ7.T37168Gr   1996   [Fic]—dc20   95-10423   CIP   AC

Published by The Millbrook Press, Inc.
2 Old New Milford Road
Brookfield, Connecticut 06804

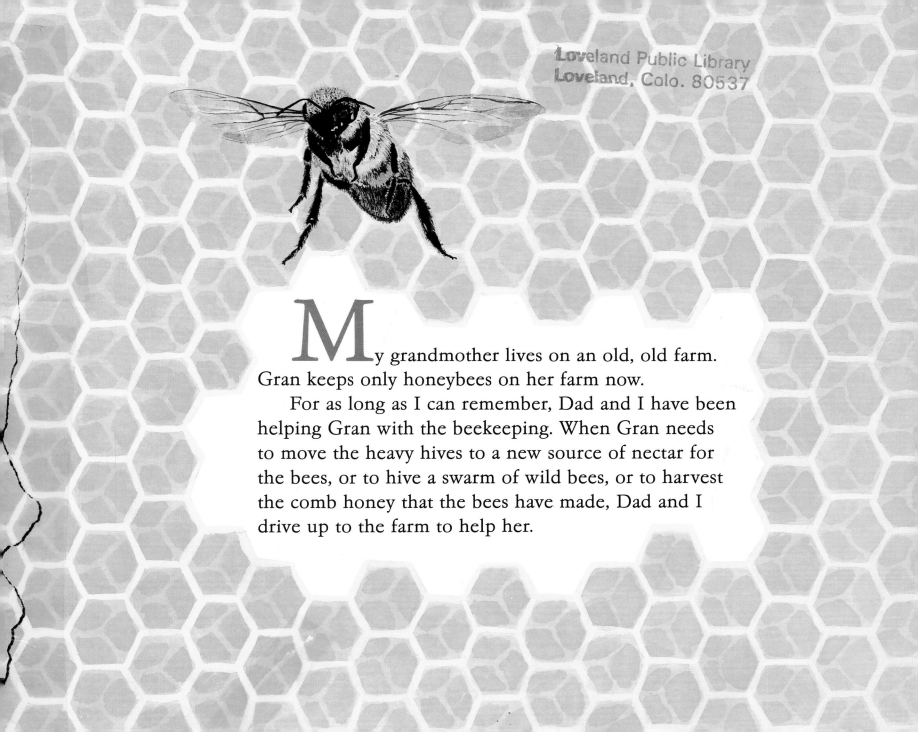

My grandmother lives on an old, old farm. Gran keeps only honeybees on her farm now.

For as long as I can remember, Dad and I have been helping Gran with the beekeeping. When Gran needs to move the heavy hives to a new source of nectar for the bees, or to hive a swarm of wild bees, or to harvest the comb honey that the bees have made, Dad and I drive up to the farm to help her.

"Getting close now," says Dad as we turn from the highway onto the gravel road. Gran's farm is the last one, farthest up the road and tucked away in its own hollow. Soon I see the cluster of farm buildings and then Gran, leaning on her cane, watching for us from her front porch.

Gran greets me with a smile. "Jessie,"
she says. Her honey-white hair tickles my neck
as I hug her hello.

"Gran," I ask, "Is today a honey harvest?"

"Last honey harvest *this* summer," she says.

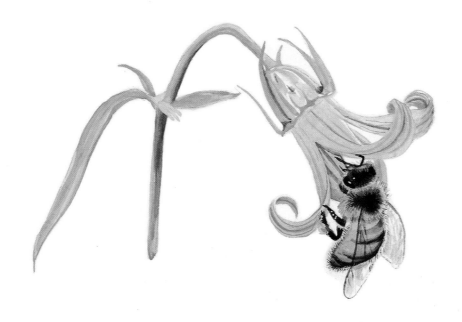

Walk together into the house. Gran's house is close with the smell of honey. And it is filled with beekeeping things. Every surface holds spare hive parts, tools, blocks of beeswax, and the little boxes and jars full of comb honey that the bees make and Gran sells. "Handy this way," she always says.

Gran fills two cups with coffee and sets them on the table. Dad finds a place for the honey cake we've brought.

"Wait!" I say. "What about spring water?"

"I saved that chore for you, Jessie," Gran says.

The spring water comes into the house through a pipe. But I always think it tastes better direct from the spring. I find a pail and run out the back door and along the path to the springhouse. When I bend to dip the pail into the water, I feel the cool springhouse air brush my skin. I take a sip. The water is cold and sweet as ever.

After we eat, Dad gathers what we need from around the house. We load Gran's pickup with our gear and a container of lemonade I make with the spring water.

"Hold on tight," Dad says. He lets me sit in the back of the pickup for the drive across the farm to the beeyard.

Gran's farm is so old that it is all woods now. The trees reach around the house and barn and stretch up and up to the top of the hollow. From my spot in the truck bed, I look up and see the branches arching over the road. It's almost like driving through a tunnel.

I like the farm this way. But Gran say that besides the forest flowers, her bees use nectar from apple blossoms, as well as from field crops like clover and buckwheat. In the early spring she puts the hives near her neighbors' orchards. This time of year, the edges of the fields are better for the bees.

"A mite ornery," Gran says, listening to the bees buzzing in the beeyard.

"Why are they ornery, Gran?" I ask.

"Maybe they know we're fixing to rob them," she answers.

Bees make more honey than they can really use. Even though Gran always leaves them plenty for their own needs, bees naturally defend their stores of honey. To protects ourselves from stings, Dad and I put on bee veils and gloves.

Even so, I'm a little scared of the ornery bees, so I close my sleeves and pant legs with rubber bands. But Gran never wears a veil or gloves or uses rubber bands.

"Gran, aren't you afraid of getting stung?" I once asked her.

"I'm too old for the bees to bother with," she told me, with a wink. But I notice that when Gran works with her bees, she moves slowly and she speaks softly. Plus, she always uses the bee smoker. Smoke doesn't hurt the bees. It just somehow slows them down.

Gran fires up the smoker with a twist of newspaper and some bits of rag, then pumps the bellows a few times. Now it will smolder all afternoon.

Gran props her cane against a hive. She aims the smoker at the hive entrance and puffs some smoke inside. In a few minutes she opens the hive, and puffs a little more smoke in at the bees. They are nice and quiet now.

Gran lifts out a frame full with honey. The bees cling, almost covering it. Gently, so as not to hurt her bees, Gran brushes them off the honeycomb with her soft-bristled bee brush.

Each of Gran's hives is home to something like fifty thousand or more bees. Every hive has one queen. There are a few male bees, called drones, who mate with the queen so she can lay eggs. But by far, most of the bees that Gran brushes off the honeycomb are female worker bees. Worker bees care for the young, collect flower nectar, and make the honey.

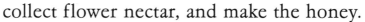

Gran hands the honey-laden frames to Dad and me. Slowly we move from hive to hive, harvesting honey.

The day is getting warmer and the afternoon air feels as slow and sticky as the honey we are gathering. Gran sets down her bee smoker. She leans on her cane.

"Plumb wore out," she says. So we rest on the truck's tailgate. Dad passes around the lemonade. A few bees circle us, brought by the smell of the honey in the truck. But they soon give up and fly off in search of flower nectar.

I've been trying to figure something out. "Gran, what do bees do during the winter, when there are no flowers?"

"Bee life changes," says Gran. "Instead of flying off to get nectar, the bees stay in the hive. When the weather gets cold, they barely move. But put your ear to the hive and you'll hear a low hum.

"When spring comes, that hive bursts into life," she continues. "The old bees that have overwintered die, and the new young bees take over the work of the hive. Year after year, certain sure."

It's late when we finish with the hives and bring in the honey. Dad and I move some of Gran's bee stuff out of the way and make supper, with biscuits for the new honey.

In the morning we put up the comb honey that we harvested from the hives. We separate the honeycomb from the wooden frame, cut it in chunks, and tip it into jars. Later, Gran will scrape the bits of beeswax from the frames to make them ready to use again next season.

Gran is polishing the last jars clean and shiny.

"There's a swarm of wild bees in the barn," she says.

"In the barn?" That's an odd place for bees to settle. Gran usually finds swarms outside in trees. And I know from Gran that this is late in the year for bees to swarm. Swarming usually happens at the peak of the spring honey flow, when there may be too many bees for a hive.

I'm curious about this swarm. I look at Dad. I know we have to leave for home soon, but I ask anyway. "Can I go see it?"

"Go ahead," he says. "I'll finish up here."

Inside, the barn is dusty, and striped with sunshine coming through the gaps in the wall. Gran's barn hasn't sheltered farm animals for many years. But I always think I can feel their warmth. I look in each empty stall.

"Milk cow on that side," says Gran. "And a mule or two over here."

Gran lowers herself onto a box while I climb up to look at the bees. They are clustered on a loose board beside the door to one of the old stalls. I'm not wearing my bee veil, so I'm afraid to get very close, but I can see that these bees have started to build comb.

That means they are planning to stay. But the the spot they have chosen is too open to wind and weather to be a good home.

I've seen Gran hive wild bees. The first part is the only tricky bit. Gran has to find the queen among the thousands of bees.

Queens are just a little longer and slenderer than the workers. Once Gran finds her, the rest is simple. She sets the queen at the entrance to an empty hive. The queen goes right into it. They like dark, secure places. The rest of the bees follow the queen, as bees will, straight into the hive.

When I climb down to tell Gran about the bees, she's asleep.

I sit on the box next to Gran and wait. I listen to Gran's humming breath, a low humming that reminds me of bees.

Pretty soon a stripe of sun reaches Gran's closed eyes and she wakes up.

"Gran," I say, "These bees are building comb, but this late in the summer they're not likely to make enough honey to last them through the winter."

Gran nods her head.

"They might not survive the cold without a hive to protect them, Gran."

She nods again.

"Gran," I say, "These bees need someone to take care of them. I think we can hive this swarm."

Gran smiles. "When you come to the farm again, Jessie, we'll hive these bees. And this time you'll help me find the queen."

About the author and illustrator

Mary Thompson's background in children's books is unusual in that she works as both an author and an illustrator. She is the author and illustrator of *My Brother Mathew*, the illustrator of *My Johnny Appleseed*, and now she is the author of *Gran's Bees*. She lives in State College, Pennsylvania.

Donna Peterson studied both art and biology at the University of Hartford in Connecticut. Her specialty is natural history illustration and she has contributed to a number of publications including *Weekly Reader*. *Gran's Bees* is her first children's book. She lives in Wethersfield, Connecticut.

GARDENING WITH ROSES

GARDENING WITH ROSES

DESIGNING WITH EASY-CARE CLIMBERS, RAMBLERS & SHRUBS

JUDITH C. MCKEON

FRIEDMAN/FAIRFAX
PUBLISHERS

A FRIEDMAN/FAIRFAX BOOK

© 1997 by Michael Friedman Publishing Group, Inc.

Library of Congress Cataloging-in-Publication Data

McKeon, Judith C.
        Gardening with roses : designing with easy-care climbers, ramblers,
& shrubs / Judith C. McKeon.
            p.   cm.
    Includes index.
    ISBN 1-56799-396-6 (hardcover)
    1. Roses.   2. Rose culture. 3. Roses—Varieties.   I. Title.
SB411.M329   1997
635.9'33372—dc20   96-36146

Editor: Susan Lauzau
Art Director: Jeff Batzli
Layout Designer: Robbi Firestone
Photography Editor: Karen L. Barr
Production Director: Karen Matsu Greenberg
Illustrations by Jennifer Markson and Susan Kemnitz

Color separations by Colourscan Overseas Co. Pte Ltd.
Printed and bound in Great Britain by
Butler & Tanner Ltd, Frome and London

2 4 6 8 10 9 7 5 3 1

For bulk purchases and special sales, please contact:
Friedman/Fairfax Publishers
Attention: Sales Department
15 West 26th Street
New York, New York 10010
212/685-6610   FAX 212/685-1307

Visit our website:
http://www.metrobooks.com

To my mother, Catherine Rush McKeon

CONTENTS

INTRODUCTION

OPPOSITE: *White roses add a touch of elegance to a mixed border and complement the crisp foliage of a white-edged hosta and the snowy flowers of lupines, irises, and lilies.*

❀

The queen of flowers typically receives mixed reviews from gardeners: cherished by some for her fragrance, charm, and elegance, she is scorned by others as a troublesome beauty. A persistent collective memory of prim Victorian rose gardens bids unwitting gardeners to create quarantined beds of glorious, but alas, often defoliated hybrid teas. In other cases roses are deemed too difficult to grow (save for the tenacious *Rosa multiflora*), and the queen is simply exiled from Eden. But a compromise may be found in the increasingly popular relaxed gardening styles. Indeed, the cottage garden tradition—in which fragrant, easy-care roses mingle with perennials, wildflowers, and old-fashioned kitchen herbs—is slowly catching the fancy of home gardeners.

Mixing roses with perennials and other shrubs allows roses to show off their virtues while downplaying their flaws. In late spring and early summer the garden will be filled with the color and fragrance of roses, and when the blooms fade, other plants can step in and take center stage.

❀

When the rose is combined creatively with other plants her virtues—scented flowers, recurrent bloom, and colorful fruits—are enhanced, while her imperfections, especially leaf problems, are attractively concealed. A lavish underplanting of perennials offers sumptuous drifts that flow around the rose's sometimes denuded canes like majestic skirts. In the mixed border, companion plants provide a setting of contrasting color and texture, against which the rose's magnificent blooms magically unfold. As part of the seasonal pageant that is the garden, the rose offers her green mantle as a backdrop for the tapestry of summer flowers, and her encore performance in late summer and autumn provides enchanting blossoms until hard frost.

ABOVE, FROM LEFT TO RIGHT: *'Stanwell Perpetual'*, Rosa hugonis, *and 'Carefree Wonder'*
❁

As more and more home gardeners abandon chemical pesticides and rigorous, high-maintenance regimes in favor of organic gardening techniques, our image of garden roses as perfect, long-stemmed beauties is slowly fading. We're replacing that somewhat idealized image with a more realistic appreciation of the rose as a versatile ornamental shrub. Like other flowering shrubs, roses are a gregarious, diverse group that mingle effortlessly with perennials in the mixed border and provide a substantial background for all manner of ornamental plants.

Most gardeners want roses that are both beautiful and trouble-free, and you can find many wonderful, easy-care shrub roses among both antique and modern types. There has recently been a spirited renaissance in heirloom rose varieties, and likewise there is a renewed faith in modern no-fuss landscape roses. But wading through the wealth of rose varieties available on the market can be a bit daunting. What's important is finding some care-free roses that grow well in your garden and that you can enjoy without a lot of hassle.

Easy-care roses are available in every habit, color, and size. There are hardy and reliable climbers, ramblers, specimen shrubs, hedges, and groundcovers. Some are well suited to rockeries or wall gardens, and the smaller types make excellent container plants for the balcony or patio. Many grow into graceful shrubs that are at home in the herb, kitchen, or cottage garden. Whatever your garden style, there's sure to be a rose tailor-made for you, and as you leaf through this book you're sure to find dozens of practical ideas for adding the grandeur of roses to your garden.

UNDERSTANDING THE LANGUAGE OF ROSES

OPPOSITE: *The climbing rose 'Eden' covers a fence with its abundant, fragrant blooms, creating a beautiful and effective screen.*

❁

An important ancestor to modern ramblers, Rosa multiflora is a rampant scrambler that produces huge panicles of single, fragrant flowers followed by small red hips.

❀

Understanding the terms that rosarians use to classify roses and being familiar with the different types of easy-care varieties available make selecting the right rose for your garden much simpler. Here we'll focus on the basic evolution of the rose and give you an easy way to remember where a particular rose variety fits into the classification system.

Classified according to their ancestry, roses are divided into two main groups: old garden roses and modern roses. Antique roses—which includes all of the classes in existence before 1867—and species, or wild, roses belong to the group known as old garden roses. Among these are many lovely shrub roses for home gardens.

The hybrid tea rose, developed from China roses and Victorian hybrid perpetuals and introduced in the 1860s, marks the advent of the age of modern roses. This group includes all classes developed since 1867. Although the hybrid tea is the most popular of all roses, especially as a cut flower, its maintenance requirements disqualify it as an easy-care rose. But even without the hybrid teas, the diversity of modern rose classes is staggering, for included in this group are ramblers, climbers, miniatures, groundcovers, and shrubs. Among these modern classes you will discover some of the best care-free roses for the home garden.

OLD GARDEN ROSES

Old garden roses, which include the species roses, are further divided into two categories. Gallica, damask, alba, centifolia, and moss roses are all derived from a common ancestor, *Rosa gallica*, and are, for the most part, once-blooming. China roses and the China-influenced roses of the nineteenth century make up the other group. These are mostly repeat-flowering, and include the period roses China, Bourbon, Noisette, perpetual damask, hybrid perpetual, and tea roses.

An early China-influenced antique rose introduced in 1817, 'Blush Noisette' bears clusters of deep pink buds that open to dainty, cupped, clear pink flowers.

In 1800 Joséphine of France painstakingly assembled the first collection of roses in the Western world, and since that time rose lovers in each generation have preserved some of the old garden roses. Even with this dedication to saving old-fashioned roses, some varieties have been lost, and these rare roses are now being sought in cemeteries, monasteries, period gardens, old homesteads, and nurseries throughout Europe and North America. Many gardeners have contributed to the effort, and a revival of old garden roses continues to generate interest as gardening becomes more and more popular as a pastime.

Our renewed appreciation for old-fashioned flowers and informal gardening styles has brought increased interest in the fragrant, long-lived old garden roses. With perfected organic gardening techniques at their fingertips, gardeners are drawn to easy-care heirloom roses more than ever before. Let's take a look at the major classes of old garden roses and discover some easy-care individuals that are well suited to the home garden.

Species Roses

Species roses are among the easiest roses to grow because most are simply indestructible. They can be grown either as shrubs or as scramblers, and are valued for their delicate single flowers and colorful hips. They look attractive with full-flowered heirloom roses, other flowering shrubs, and perennial companions in an informal setting. Many tolerate high shade from deciduous trees and can be satisfactorily

grown at the edge of a woodland. Some of the best roses for this purpose include red-leaved rose (*Rosa glauca*), a superb specimen shrub cultivated for its distinctive foliage; the rugged and free-flowering Scotch briar (*R. spinosissima*); and sweetbriar, or eglantine rose (*R. eglanteria*), which is cherished for its fragrant, apple-scented foliage. Species roses tend to be tough landscape plants and are useful in spots where more delicate roses might fail; sites in blazing sun, dry city gardens, and hot spots near paving are all difficult planting situations where resilient species roses will fare well. The rugosa rose (*R. rugosa*), also known as sea tomato, thrives on sand dunes, and so makes a lovely addition to a seaside garden.

Species roses such as sweetbriar, with its apple-scented leaves; the dog rose (*R. canina*), which produces a spectacular crop of hips rich in vitamin C; and fragrant damask rose (*R. damascena* var. *trigintipetala*), which yields attar from its pressed petals, naturally find a place with companion culinary and ornamental herbs. That's why species roses are so often integrated into flower gardens, cottage gardens, and gardens of historical houses. Few gardeners realize that roses are shrubby herbs that have traditionally found a home in the herb or physic garden, where their useful medicinal, culinary, and perfume qualities were well appreciated.

Species roses are sometimes grown purely for their ornamental value. Wingthorn four-petal rose (*R. sericea* var. *pteracantha*) is armed with spectacular thorns of translucent scarlet and looks lovely in all seasons. Father Hugo's rose (*R. hugonis*), also known as the golden rose of China, is admired for its lemon yellow blooms and exquisite fern-leaf foliage.

Wild scramblers can be planted to create an impenetrable mass of briars or as groundcovers for steep slopes, but they can also be trained to cover unsightly structures, grow into trees, and drape walls and fences. The vigorous, scrambling Helen rose (*R. helenae*) stretches to 20 feet (6m) and carries masses of small, white, scented flowers in large trusses followed by small, red hips. The prairie rose (*R. setigera*) is a tough North American native that can be wrapped around a sturdy pillar or trained as a colorful groundcover. In late summer, the reddish canes are studded with pink flowers, which are followed by small, red hips; foliage turns an attractive scarlet-bronze in autumn.

Once-Blooming Old Garden Roses

Gallica, damask, alba, centifolia, and moss roses originated in Europe and evolved from a complex lineage involving a common ancestor, *Rosa gallica*. The old roses bloom in early summer with no repeat flowering (except for 'Autumn Damask', *R. damascena* var. *bifera*). Most are extremely hardy, disease-resistant, prickly shrubs that grow and thrive with little attention from the gardener. They range in height from 3 to 6 feet (1 to 1.8m) tall and their flower colors range from pure white through blush pink, deep pink, and rose to crimson, purple, and magenta. Bicolored and striped flowers, which are beloved for their novel effect, are found chiefly among gallicas.

The once-blooming old roses are exceptionally long-lived, and among them are many beautiful low-maintenance shrubs for modern gardens. They blend easily with other shrubs and perennials in mixed borders; many make excellent screens and hedges. Set against an evergreen background, their massive flower displays are showstoppers in early summer, then they recede into the green background when not in bloom.

❧Gallica Roses

Gallica roses make excellent compact garden shrubs. They are easy-care roses noted for their extreme hardiness, disease resistance, medium-green foliage, and tidy flowers held upright on bristly stems. Rich, velvety blooms in shades of deep pink to crimson, burgundy, violet, and plum are characteristic, and some cultivars have charming bicolored, striped, and brightly splashed flowers.

Some recommended gallicas are 'Apothecary's Rose', also known as *Rosa gallica* var. *officinalis*, and its striped sport 'Rosa Mundi', also known as *R. gallica* var. *versicolor*. Cultivars with rich, reddish plum or purple flowers include 'Sissinghurst Castle', 'Alain Blanchard', 'Charles de Mills', and 'Superb Tuscan'. These gallicas are particularly striking when set off by silver-leaved plants; try planting them with perennial companions such as artemisia, santolina, and lamb's ears. Gallica roses tolerate some light shade, and you can create a lovely seasonal garden picture by interplanting them with wildflowers, wild shrubs, and companion perennials at the edge of a woodland. Hardy to Zone 3, gallica roses offer gardeners many tough and beautiful varieties.

'Apothecary's Rose' is among the best of the old roses for small gardens. It makes a superb mass planting or low hedge.

❧Damask Roses

Because the damask rose is associated with intense fragrance, its name conjures up thoughts of soft pink blooms perfuming the air on a warm summer day. Damask roses are the chief source of essential oil, or attar, which is extracted mainly from the fresh-picked flowers of 'Kazanlik', *Rosa damascena* var. *trigintipetala*. Traditionally produced in Bulgaria, India, Persia, Turkey, and Morocco, attar is used in making rose water, as well as perfume. The petals of damask roses—most notably 'Celsiana' and 'Ispahan'—can also be collected and dried for use as an ingredient in potpourri.

A diverse class, damask roses form vigorous, upright or lax shrubs and have very thorny canes that are covered with downy gray-green foliage. Robust, disease-resistant, and free-flowering, damask shrubs are taller than their compact gallica parents. Flower colors include shades from pure white and soft tints of blush pink to clear and deep pink. There are a few bicolored damasks as well.

Like gallica roses, to which they are closely related, damasks are very old, and only a small number of cultivars have survived. Damask roses are sun-lovers, whose perfumed flowers qualify them as excellent candidates for the herb garden, cottage garden, and sunny mixed border. Popular damask cultivars include 'Celsiana', 'Blush Damask', 'Madame Zoetmans', and 'Madame Hardy', which is considered the most perfect of all rose flowers. For small gardens, compact 'Leda' and 'Petite Lizette' are choice damask specimens. Often selected for the excellent perfume of their flowers, damask roses are also moderately disease-resistant and are hardy to Zone 3.

Alba Roses

White, or alba, roses are vigorous, upright, bushy shrubs that have distinctive bluish leaves. They are easy to grow and are the most rugged, hardy, disease-free, and shade-tolerant of all the old roses, making them the perfect choice for novice rose gardeners. Ancestors of alba roses include Shakespeare's briar rose, the dog rose (*Rosa canina*), and damask roses. As the name of this class suggests, flower color is restricted to pure white and soft tints of blush pink. Like gallicas and damasks, alba roses are very old. Today, there are only a few albas available, but all of them are beautiful additions to the garden.

Some notable members of this aristocratic group are 'Félicité Parmentier', 'Konigin von Dane-mark', 'Maiden's Blush', and 'Celestial'. All of these shrubs are easy to grow and look particularly lovely when they are mixed with blue-flowered ornamental herbs such as lavender, catnip, and salvia.

TOP: *The damask rose 'Celsiana' exudes a delicious fragrance.*

❁

ABOVE: *'Konigin von Danemark', also known as 'Queen of Denmark', is an aristocratic alba rose admired by gardeners since its debut in 1826.*

❁

The scented petals of these and other alba roses are ideal when dried as an ingredient in potpourri. 'Alba Semi-Plena', 'Madame Legras de St. Germain', and 'Madame Plantier' make particularly good subjects for training as pillar roses or short climbers because of their floppy habits.

Quick to get established in the garden, care-free alba roses produce a wealth of fragrant flowers with minimal care. Since they're hardy to Zone 3, they can even be grown successfully in cold regions.

Centifolia Roses

Prized for their full, very double, and extremely fragrant flowers, centifolia roses were considered the most beautiful of all flowers at their zenith in the eighteenth century. Evolved from a complex blend of gallica, damask, and alba roses—with a few Asian species roses, including the musk rose (*Rosa moschata*), thrown in—the centifolia rose reached its pinnacle of fame as a florist flower in Holland, largely through the efforts of seventeenth- and eighteenth-century Dutch breeders. Often featured in the Dutch Masters' paintings of the period, the centifolia rose came to be known as "the rose of the painters." The English dubbed centifolias cabbage roses, but this nickname does not accurately describe the elegant, chalice-shaped, many-petaled form of centifolia blooms.

Dried petals of fragrant centifolia flowers form the major ingredient in traditional potpourris. At Munstead Wood, Gertrude Jekyll's home in England, centifolia and damask petals were collected by the pound for her biannual potpourri production. In Provence, in southern France, an essence extracted from the petals of centifolia roses is used as an ingredient in fine French perfumes. It is from this association that centifolia roses came to be known as Provence roses.

Centifolia roses are substantial shrubs and generally fill a background position in the garden, although there are some compact and miniature cultivars. They are exceptionally hardy and robust, and resist disease moderately well. When in bloom, these graceful shrubs appear heavy with masses of full, nodding flowers typically in shades of pink. Most benefit from pegging or training on a fence to manage their long, arching canes; 'Centifolia', 'Fantin-Latour', and 'La Noblesse' are all excellent candidates for these treatments. For small gardens, the compact 'Rose de Meux' and 'Pompon de Bourgogne' are perfect for edging or for the front of the border. Centifolia roses are recommended for northern gardens because they are hardy to Zone 4.

OPPOSITE: *'Fantin-Latour',
an old-fashioned favorite, has
enchanting, blush-tinted
flowers composed of as many
as two hundred petals.*

Moss Roses

Moss roses originated as sports, or natural mutations, of centifolia and damask roses. Moss roses take their name from the resinous, green, mossy glands that thickly cover their buds and exude a balsam scent when brushed. Centifolia roses share their characteristics of hardiness, vigor, rich fragrance, and summer bloom with their moss rose offshoots.

'Communis', or 'Common Moss', also known as 'Old Pink Moss', is probably the original moss rose sport of centifolia and has been cultivated for at least three hundred years. It endures as the best and most cherished of the moss roses; its white sport, 'Shailer's White Moss', flowers over a long period and exudes an exquisite perfume. Other recommended moss roses include 'Comtesse de Murinais', 'Striped Moss', and 'Nuits de Young', also known as 'Old Black'.

China-Influenced Old Garden Roses

The breeding and cultivation of roses have been integral to Chinese gardening for five thousand years. Through selection and hybridization, Chinese breeders enhanced the repeat-blooming character of *Rosa chinensis* and produced hybrids noted for their continuous bloom. When official trade routes opened between Europe and Asia, China roses were imported to the West, appearing around 1800. Before the arrival of China roses, Western gardeners cultivated only once-blooming species roses and old European roses descended from *R. gallica*; of these, only 'Autumn Damask' provided some coveted repeat bloom. With the arrival of everblooming China roses, a Western breeding revolution began, and novelty roses soon featured the trait of repeat-flowering. Precursors to modern roses, these period roses include the China, Bourbon, Noisette, damask perpetual, and hybrid perpetual classes. Everblooming tea-scented roses, descended from another China rose, the tea rose (*R. odorata*), also came into favor during the nineteenth century. China roses are a primary ancestor of our modern hybrid tea roses.

These China-influenced roses heralded the modern age of Western garden and florist roses. As the reputation of these period roses increased, the once-blooming old roses declined in popularity. Hybridizing increased in a frenzied response to a demand for novelty roses. Often, hardiness and fragrance were sacrificed in the race for roses that would repeat their bloom. Each new class was enthusiastically bred and interbred, mostly by French hybridizers, and resulted in the myriad culti-vars listed in nursery catalogs of the time.

China-influenced roses are not as hardy as once-blooming old roses, and, like their modern suc-cessors, they may be either disease-resistant or disease prone. Included in this group of period roses are many exquisite individuals worth growing. China-influenced roses should find a home in every garden where the climate is suitable, from Zones 5 to 10.

Choice garden specimens include the hardy damask perpetual roses 'Rose de Rescht', 'Four Seasons', and 'Jacques Cartier'; China roses 'Mutabalis', 'Hermosa', and miniature 'Roulettii'; the excellent climbing tea roses 'Sombreuil' and 'Gloire de Dijon'; everblooming compact Bourbons 'Souvenir de la Malmaison' and tall 'Honorine de Brabant'; dainty-flowered 'Blush Noisette' and vig-orous climbing 'Madame Alfred Carrière'; and the thornless hybrid perpetual 'Reine des Violettes'.

In 1902, Gertrude Jekyll named 'Madame Alfred Carrière' the best white climber; among antique roses, this vigorous, repeat-blooming Noisette rose still claims the title.

China Roses

China roses are rarely out of bloom and typically produce cupped flowers that deepen in color with age rather than fading. Bushes are relatively small, wiry, and airy, with smooth interstems and shiny, pointed leaves that are tinged red when they emerge. For best effect, blend China roses into mixed borders; surround them with perennials and herbs, and give them a background of larger flowering shrubs, including other old or modern roses. China roses lend an air of enchantment throughout the season with their small cupped blooms, and they can always be counted on to give a bit of flower color to the autumn garden. Fragrance is variable and not as intense as in other old roses, but when they're underplanted with dianthus or sweet William, this occasional imperfection goes unnoticed.

From the famous quartet of China roses that contributed their repeat-blooming character to modern roses, only 'Old Blush' is still commonly grown in gardens. 'Old Blush' is known by many names, including 'Parson's Pink China', 'Common Monthly', and 'Old Pink Monthly', which describe its pink flowers and continuous-blooming nature. Some of the best Chinas include 'Mutabilis', 'Hermosa', and dwarf 'Roulettii', a progenitor of modern miniature roses.

Damask Perpetual Roses

Damask perpetual, or Portland, roses are the unsung heroes of the rose world and they make excellent care-free shrubs for small gardens. Derived from 'Autumn Damask', which contributes repeat flowering and a damask scent, damask perpetual roses are compact, bushy plants that bloom abundantly in late spring and again in autumn. Undoubtedly, some gallica genes are mixed in, which account for the bristly stems, crimson shades, and hardiness of damask perpetuals, and there may be some China rose influence as well. What is important for gardeners, however, is that damask perpetual roses are among the easiest and most rewarding of the old roses to grow.

Damask perpetual roses contribute fragrance and a long flowering season to the mixed border. The compact bushes associate well with other antique or modern roses and with perennial companions. If you only have space in your garden for a few rosebushes, choose one from among these humble champions: 'Jacques Cartier'; 'Comte de Chambord'; 'Four Seasons'; and compact 'Rose de Rescht'. Damask perpetual roses are hardy to Zone 5.

OPPOSITE: *Few roses of any period are as sweetly scented as the great 1881 Bourbon rose 'Madame Isaac Pereire'. Typically trained as a short climber or wall shrub, it looks beautiful paired with dark blue or purple perennials such as delphinium, larkspur, salvia, or Siberian iris.*

BELOW: *'Old Blush', or 'Common Monthly', is one of the "parent" China roses that contributed its everblooming character to modern roses.*

🌹Bourbon Roses

Bourbon roses originated from a chance cross between the China rose 'Old Blush' and 'Autumn Damask'. Bourbon blooms are typically large, cupped, many-petaled, and very fragrant. 'Madame Isaac Pereire' and thornless 'Zéphirine Drouhin' are suitable for training as short climbers, attaining 5 to 6 feet (1.5 to 1.8m) in height. Plant a large-flowered clematis, such as sky blue 'Will Goodwin', to weave through the rose; this winning combination creates a stunning show in early summer, adds summer floral color, and hides the naked canes of these roses, which are prone to black spot. For disease-resistant Bourbons, choose tall 'Honorine de Brabant' or the exquisite, compact Bourbon 'Souvenir de la Malmaison'.

🌹Noisette Roses

Rarely out of bloom, 'Nastarana' produces pure white single flowers with yellow stamens and, like other Noisette roses, is often trained as a climber.

Noisette roses were developed in the United States from a cross between China and musk roses. They add soft yellow or apricot to the color range of the antique rose palette. Most produce trusses of small flowers in hues of soft white, lemon, or pale pink on wiry, upright bushes. Some of the taller Noisettes, such as 'Blush Noisette' and 'Nastarana' can be trained against a south-facing wall. If your

plants suffer winter injury in marginal northern gardens, then grow Noisettes as small upright shrubs, just as you would floribundas. Like their China parents, most Noisette roses are rarely out of bloom; many make excellent climbers in Zones 7 to 10. A few climbers, such as 'Madame Alfred Carrière' can be grown on a protected wall in Zone 6. Noisettes are true sun-lovers.

🌹Tea Roses

Very fragrant forms of the China group, tea roses were developed from crosses between *Rosa chinensis* (China rose) and *R. gigantea* (a giant Chinese rose that climbs to 50 feet [15m]). One of these crosses produced *Rosa* × *odorata,* also known as 'Hume's Blush Tea-scented China', an early tea rose. Like the Noisettes, tea roses bring soft yellow and apricot colors to the antique rose palette. With urn-shaped buds opening to high-centered flowers on long stems, tea roses

The hardiest of the climbing tea roses, 'Sombreuil' bears abundant, scented, creamy blooms. Weave a small-flowered clematis through the canes of this rose for subtle contrast.

were much loved in Victorian times and were often worn as lapel flowers. The familiar flower form of the tea rose was transmitted to its hybrid tea offspring. Tea roses are extremely tender and typically flourish in warm climates (Zones 7 to 10), or in greenhouses as potted plants. The relatively vigorous climbing teas 'Sombreuil' and 'Gloire de Dijon' are worth growing on a protected wall in Zone 6.

Hybrid Perpetual Roses

Introduced in the 1830s, hybrid perpetuals were bred from a complex mingling of the China-influenced classes and old European roses. The hybrid perpetual became the favorite flower of the Victorians and reigned as queen until the twentieth century, when it was succeeded by the hybrid tea rose. While the designation "perpetual" is misleading because the shrubs are not continuously in bloom, many cultivars produce late-summer flowers. They are prone to diseases and cannot be considered easy-care roses, but a few are worth growing. Damask perpetual roses played an important role in the development of the hybrid perpetuals, and their contribution is clearly shown in 'Baronne Prévost'. Other useful hybrid perpetuals include 'Vick's Caprice' and thornless 'Reine des Violettes'. Hybrid perpetual roses are hardy to Zone 5.

'Armada', a repeat-blooming modern shrub rose, makes a bold statement with its huge sprays of clear pink flowers set dramatically against a backdrop of colorful ramblers.

MODERN ROSES

Asian tea roses descended from *Rosa odorata* were bred with hybrid perpetual and China roses to create continuous-blooming hybrid tea roses. The hybrid tea rose celebrated its debut sometime after 1850. 'La France' was introduced in 1867 and is considered by many to be the first hybrid tea; the year 1867 was later chosen to mark the inauguration of the modern rose era. Over the course of nearly a century, modern roses were influenced by important developments in rose breeding that set the stage for new classes of roses. The introduction of the multiflora (*R. multifolra*) and memorial (*R. wichuraiana*) roses from China in the late nineteenth century, for example, led to the creation of polyantha, rambler, and large-flowered climbing roses. Everblooming China roses continued to play an important role in modern breeding, particularly of polyantha and miniature roses. From 1867 to the mid-twentieth century, modern classes of hybrid tea, polyantha, rambler, climber, miniature, floribunda, grandiflora, and shrub roses were introduced.

Colors of roses introduced before 1900 are restricted to cool tones in shades of white, pink, and bluish-red or magenta. In modern roses the spectrum is greatly expanded to encompass the hot palette of yellow, orange, and scarlet. The color barrier was exploded by the French hybridizer Joseph Pernet-Ducher in 1900, when he successfully engineered a cross between *R. foetida* 'Persian Yellow' and a hybrid perpetual to produce the hybrid tea 'Soleil d'Or' with rich, yellow-orange blooms. The full spectrum of clear yellow, gold, and apricot to brilliant orange and flame colors is represented in twentieth-century roses.

Perfect for covering buildings and rose arches, and for growing up into trees, the rambler 'Bobbie James' produces masses of exceptionally fragrant petite blooms.

Climbers and Ramblers

Climbers and ramblers are excellent landscape choices for all gardens. Where vertical space permits, they can be trained as wall shrubs, grown on fences, and wound up pillars to create interest at several heights and to conserve space in small gardens. The ramblers and climbers so popular in today's gardens are derived primarily from wild rose scramblers, such as the multiflora and memorial roses, which were introduced from China in the late nineteenth century.

The most popular climbing rose of all time, 'American Pillar' accentuates a pergola with its distinctive carmine blooms and lends an easy grace to this English-style mixed border.

Once widely planted in hedgerows throughout North America, the exotic multiflora rose became naturalized and is now designated as a noxious weed in many states. Nevertheless, this rampant species has made important contributions to modern roses. Large, pyramidal corymbs, or clusters, of small, fragrant blooms make up the familiar flower form of multiflora rose and its offspring, polyantha and hybrid musk roses. Hybrid multiflora ramblers take care of themselves and in addition provide perfume, vigor, disease resistance, and an aptitude for tenacious scrambling.

Ramblers are vigorous—even rampant—growers that bear long, flexible canes and are generally derived from the multiflora rose and memorial rose, as well as from a few individual "scrambler" species. Ramblers are once-blooming roses and typically produce a profusion of small flowers in large trusses, or clusters, in summer. Excellent hardy and disease-resistant ramblers for the home garden include 'Chevy Chase', 'Tausendschon', 'Bobbie James', and 'Seagull'.

'Seagull' and 'Bobbie James' easily reach the second story of a house and are good candidates for training into medium-size trees. Once trained over the trunk, a rambler will pull itself up by its prickles and grow toward the light, scrambling into deciduous trees such as crab apples with ease. (See "Planting Climbers and Ramblers to Grow into Trees" on page 45.) Striking effects can be achieved when either thoughtful design or accident provides the perfect match of rambler and tree. These recommended ramblers are disease-resistant and hardy to Zone 5.

Memorial rose forms a trailing groundcover with glossy, disease-resistant leaves and single white flowers. Using memorial rose crossed with tea, hybrid tea, and polyantha roses, American hybridizer Dr. William Van Fleet—one of the pioneer breeders of ramblers and climbers—created many hybrids popular in the first quarter of the twentieth century, including 'American Pillar' and 'Dr. W. Van Fleet'. This vigorous climber, with glossy, disease-resistant foliage, produces masses of light pink, fragrant, hybrid tea–type flowers in summer.

Only nature could have improved upon this excellent climber. In 1930, a repeat-blooming sport of 'Dr. W. Van Fleet'—a shoot different from its parent—was discovered, patented, and introduced as 'New Dawn'. One of the best-known large-flowered climbers, 'New Dawn' has been extensively bred with hybrid tea and floribunda roses to create an entire tribe of reblooming, large-flowered climbers, including 'White Cockade' and 'Parade'.

Polyantha Roses

Forerunners of the modern floribunda roses, polyantha, or sweetheart, roses belong to a recognized class of small shrubs that resulted from breeding multiflora roses with China roses. One of the earliest sweetheart roses, 'Cécile Brunner', was introduced in the 1890s. Other recommended polyantha roses include 'Marie Pavie', 'Clotilde Soupert', 'Baby Faurax', 'China Doll', and 'The Fairy', which has become one of the most enduring and popular of all low-growing roses. Rarely out of bloom, polyantha rosebushes are shown to advantage when planted in groups of three or more at the front of a mixed border, where they create spots of season-long

'Climbing Cécile Brunner' easily stretches to 20 feet (6m) and blankets itself in sprays of sweetheart blooms.

color. Polyanthas behave much like herbaceous perennial drifts, and should be sheared after each flowering period. Polyantha roses are hardy to Zone 5.

❧Floribunda Roses

Vigorous and free-flowering, floribunda roses are the result of crossbreeding between polyantha roses and hybrid teas. Compact bushy shrubs produce clusters of showy blooms, many of which resemble small, high-centered hybrid tea blooms, but they also come in a flat antique style and five-petaled or single-flower forms. An excellent landscape rose for borders, beds, and hedging, floribunda roses were introduced in the 1930s.

Some floribunda roses are extremely disease-resistant and behave like easy-care shrub roses. These are the ones that most gardeners will want to choose. Classic hardy, disease-resistant varieties with single flowers in shades of pink and mauve include 'Nearly Wild', 'Betty Prior', and 'Escapade'. Some easy-to-grow flame-colored varieties are 'Sarabande', 'Impatient', and 'Playboy'; for bright yellow and peach shades, try fragrant 'Sunsprite' and 'Apricot Nectar'. Excellent white-flowered cultivars include the early floribunda 'Gruss an Aachen', 'Iceberg', and 'Class Act'. Floribunda roses are hardy to Zone 5.

❧Miniature

Miniature roses are a fascinating, diverse class that represents the rose world in microcosm. Typically, the tiny flowers resemble many-petaled hybrid tea or floribunda roses; however, old-fashioned styles of flowers are also represented, with single, semidouble, and mossy buds that open to full, old rose blooms. Some miniatures even have the wonderful fragrance associated with old roses.

Miniature roses also display a wide range of habits, including bush, mounding shrub, climber, groundcover, and standard, or tree, rose. The bush types vary in height from the micro-miniature, which stands about 10 inches (25cm) tall, to the upright long-stemmed hybrid tea style, which reaches about 2 feet (61cm) in height.

Since the introduction of 'Tom Thumb' in 1935, miniatures have gradually grown in popularity. California hybridizer Ralph Moore is an important contributor to the diversity of miniature roses—his 'Pinstripe' and 'Magic Carrousel' are reminiscent of striped gallicas and his cascading 'Sweet Chariot' bears trusses of tiny, fragrant, lavender blooms. Additional recommended cultivars include 'Cupcake', 'Black Jade', 'Debut', and 'Minnie Pearl', all of which feature exquisite hybrid tea–style flowers. 'Popcorn' and its sport 'Gourmet Popcorn' offer charming single and semidouble flowers, respectively, while the diminutive 'Cinderella' is classed as a micro-miniature. Climbing miniatures include 'Nozomi', 'Jeanne Lajoie', and 'Red Cascade', all of which also make great groundcovers.

OPPOSITE, FROM TOP TO BOTTOM: 'Nearly Wild', 'Escapade,' and 'Debut'

Care-Free Modern Shrub Roses

The catchall class known simply as "shrub roses" was designated to embrace roses that do not fit into other modern classes. Gathered under the shrub rose umbrella are many excellent disease-resistant, hardy, easy-care garden roses. Some of the distinct subclasses collected here include the lovely, fragrant hybrid musks, the tough hybrid rugosas, and the modern hybrids of species roses such as eglantine and Scotch.

Because of their hardiness, disease resistance, and free-flowering nature, rugosa and Scotch roses have been used extensively in the breeding of superior hybrid shrubs for garden and landscape use. 'Frau Dagmar Hartopp', 'Hansa', 'Blanc Double de Coubert', and 'Roseraie de l' Hay' perform admirably as specimens, hedges, screens, and drifts, and are distinguished by all-season color and fragrance. The rugosa rose and its hybrids are reliably repeat-flowering and the single-flowered forms produce superior, huge, tomato red hips.

The amorphous shrub class includes diverse habits, sizes, and flower forms, including upright bushes; loose, mounding shrubs often trained as climbers, such as hardy Kordesii shrubs; the low-growing groundcover Meidiland series; patio roses; and English roses.

Since the mid-twentieth century, when Wilhelm Kordes of Germany introduced his hardy, disease-resistant Kordes rose (*Rosa × kordesii*) and its offspring, modern breeding programs have produced a steady stream of disease-resistant, hardy, repeat-flowering shrub roses for garden and landscape use, often called "landscape roses." Easy-care, hardy landscape roses thrive and bloom

ENGLISH ROSES

Developed in Albrighton, England, by David Austen, English roses combine the fragrance and charm of gallica and damask roses with the characteristics of repeat flowering and the expanded color range of modern roses. Austen crossed the gallica 'Belle Isis' with the floribunda 'Dainty Maid' to produce 'Constance Spry' in 1961. Since then, he has raised about eighty cultivars of English roses. Notable reblooming cultivars include 'Graham Thomas', which has full, apricot-yellow blooms; 'Mary Rose', which features rose pink flowers in old rose form; 'Heritage', which bears full, cupped blooms in soft blush pink; 'Fair Bianca', which produces buds tinged with deep pink that open to creamy white, myrrh-scented flowers reminiscent of 'Madame Hardy'; 'Othello', which bears abundant crimson blooms; 'Dapple Dawn', which has charming, pink, single flowers with distinctive amber stamens; 'Windrush', which features delightful single blooms in lemon with amber stamens; and 'Wife of Bath', a bush with a growth habit similar to a floribunda, which produces soft pink, luscious blooms almost continuously.

Like the grandiflora roses they resemble, most English roses are hardy to Zone 5 with protection. Some of the once-blooming older cultivars such as 'Constance Spry' and 'Shropshire Lass' are hardy to Zone 4. The prototype 'Constance Spry' is easily trained as a spectacular climber to drape over walls and fences. All varieties bloom profusely in early summer. However, individual garden performance, including growth habit, disease resistance, and reliable repeat-flowering varies regionally. Talk with local nurseries and gardeners to find out which English roses they have the most success with or ask your local chapter of the American Rose Society for recommendations of English roses best suited for your region. Alternatively, just try the cultivars that appeal to you!

Often vigorous, upright cultivars such as 'Graham Thomas' throw tremendously long canes after the first bloom and throughout the summer when grown in North America, and gardeners find this behavior most confusing. It is a vigorous response to the hot, sunny days and warm nights in many regions of the North America, which cause bushes to react with a vegetative spurt instead of setting more flower buds, as they do in England. Manage these long canes with hard pruning; reduce canes by two thirds of their length to encourage later blooms and to maintain a tidy habit.

English roses are best displayed in small groupings of three or more plants. In mixed borders, the long canes of taller cultivars need to be controlled with hard pruning; shrubby cultivars such as 'Mary Rose' and 'Wife of Bath' are easier to integrate with companion perennials and other roses. In a position at the back of the border, flowers of tall cultivars, such as 'Graham Thomas', nod over other shrubs and can be viewed to advantage while their awkward growth habit is hidden.

ABOVE: *'Graham Thomas', named in honor of the noted English horticulturist, is one of the most popular English roses.*

with little maintenance, and they're useful in the garden for massing or for use as screens, hedges, groundcovers, pillar roses, and specimen plantings. They are typically reblooming, and in autumn some produce colorful rose hips that attract birds. These tough roses thrive with little attention from the gardener.

Many floppy and mounding shrubs of modern origin make excellent short climbing or pillar roses; these include 'Dortmund', 'Parkdirektor Riggers', and 'Westerland'.

The Kordes rose was also used in breeding Canadian Explorer roses at Agriculture Canada in Ottawa; they offer extreme hardiness and repeat-flowering in shades of deep pink and crimson. Those suitable for training as climbers include 'John Cabot', 'John Davis', 'Henry Kelsey', and 'William Baffin'. Because the Canadian Explorer roses are hardy to Zone 3, northern gardeners can create romantic garden scenes using these superior hardy roses as climbers on arbors, walls, and pillars.

Hybrid Tea Roses

The most exalted of the modern roses, the hybrid tea's ancestry includes hybrid perpetual, China, and tea roses. Elegant, urn-shaped buds open into large, full, high-centered flowers carried on long stems. Garden cultivars produce flowers continuously from late spring through frost, and bushes typically grow 3 to 6 feet (1 to 1.8m) tall in an upright habit. Represented by more than seven thousand cultivars, the hybrid tea is the world's favorite rose for exhibition and florist use, and it is the progenitor of several other major modern classes.

The hybrid tea 'Rio Samba', an All-America Rose Selection for 1993, has a good rating for disease resistance.

Although large-flowered hybrid tea roses are the most readily available, they are rarely the best choice for the low-maintenance gardener. They require a lot of care and are notoriously prone to diseases. In addition, their stiff upright habit makes them difficult to blend with informal perennials and shrubs. If you must have them, select only the most disease-resistant cultivars (see the chart "Disease-Resistant Large-Flowered Hybrid Tea Roses") and be prepared to treat them several times with fungicides, beginning when they first leaf out in early spring.

Exquisite 'Dainty Bess', whose old-fashioned single flowers associate splendidly with perennial companions, is one notable exception. Fragrant pink flowers are large, have only five petals, and are filled with maroon stamens; upright canes reach 4 to 5 feet (1.2 to 1.5m). 'Dainty Bess' does require several fungicide treatments beginning in early spring to maintain the foliage that provides the energy for repeat bloom.

DISEASE-RESISTANT LARGE-FLOWERED HYBRID TEA ROSES

'Love'—red blooms with white reverse (petals are white on the outside and red on the inside)

'Chrysler Imperial'—magenta-red flowers that are extremely fragrant

'Gold Medal'—golden yellow blooms

'Marjike Koopman'—deep pink flowers with a light fragrance

'Fragrant Cloud'—red-orange, extremely fragrant blooms

'Rio Samba'—yellow-orange bicolored blooms

CHAPTER TWO

GROWING EASY-CARE ROSES

OPPOSITE: *An easy way to get started with care-free roses is to add some climbers to your garden. They can be trained on trees, pillars, arches, or existing structures to create a romantic vertical accent and a feeling of lushness in the garden.*

Like other flowering shrubs, easy-care roses can be grown in the home garden with minimal care from the gardener. Flowering shrubs such as butterfly bush require some pruning and deadheading to maintain their best appearance; viburnums benefit from an occasional thinning to rejuvenate the bush; and azaleas flower better with an annual application of fertilizer. Care-free roses have similar maintenance requirements and thrive best with some simple practices in your garden. This chapter gives you the basic information you need to maintain healthy, productive rosebushes.

Sweetheart rose 'Marie Pavie' and perennial companions thrive in a sunny bed edged with boxwood, while the vigorous scrambler Rosa multiflora var. carnea crowns an arched entrance.

SITE

Because roses, like tomatoes and marigolds, are sun lovers, they will thrive more readily in a hot spot than in a shaded area. A sunny situation is especially important for the repeat-blooming types, which benefit from at least a half day, or six hours, of sunlight. This ample supply of rays provides the energy required for abundant flower displays. If you plant repeat- and everblooming roses in shady areas, you'll be disappointed with their performance, for your roses will grow tall and spindly with only a few flowers.

If your garden is shaded by deciduous trees, try cutting some of the lower limbs from the trees or opening the canopy by selective pruning to provide more sunlight. Instead of planting roses that are sure to fail, grow species and alba roses that flower in late spring or early summer and tolerate dappled light or high shade from deciduous trees. These easy-care roses require less summer sunlight because they set flower buds in spring before leaves emerge on shade trees. However, even tough species roses do not tolerate heavy shade from maple trees, evergreen trees, or a site in the shadow of your house or garage.

Avoid low-lying areas that are wet or boggy, since roses prefer well-drained soil. If you have a sunny site that does not drain well, reclaim this spot by building berms or raised beds.

ROSES TO GROW IN DAPPLED SHADE

Species Roses

Sweetbriar rose (*Rosa eglanteria*)
Red-leaved rose (*Rosa glauca*)
Cherokee rose (*Rosa laevigata*)
New England shining rose (*Rosa nitida*)
Swamp rose (*Rosa palustris*)
Incense rose (*Rosa primula*)
Prairie rose (*Rosa setigera*)
Scotch rose (*Rosa spinosissima*)
Virginia rose (*Rosa virginiana*)
Memorial rose (*Rosa wichuraiana*)
Mountain rose (*Rosa woodsii*)

Hybrid Wichuraiana Climbers

'Albéric Barbier'
'Dr. W. Van Fleet'
'Silver Moon'

Ramblers

'Chevy Chase'
'Kew Rambler'
'Russelliana'
'Seagull'
'Tausendschon'
'Kiftsgate'

Hybrid Musks

'Ballerina'
'Cornelia'
'Clytemnestra'
'Felicia'
'Moonlight'
'Penelope'

Alba Roses

'Alba Semi-Plena'
'Konigin von Danemark'
'Great Maiden's Blush'
'Maiden's Blush'
'Maxima'
'Madame Legras de St. Germain'
'Madame Plantier'

Gallica Roses

'Alain Blanchard'
'Apothecary's Rose'
'Complicata'
'La Belle Sultane'
'Rosa Mundi'
'Tuscany'

Like garden vegetables, roses grow best in a rich, well-drained soil amended with lots of humus in the form of compost, manure, or Milorganite.

✿

SOIL

Once you have found a nice, sunny, well-drained location for your roses, it's a good idea to learn about the composition of your soil. With a professional soil test, you can find out the amount of essential nutrients in your soil as well as its pH, or degree of acidity or alkalinity. Large garden centers and cooperative extension services have available test kits that can then be mailed to a soil test laboratory. As an alternative, you can buy a simple test that you can perform yourself, but these kits will only tell you the pH of the soil.

On the pH scale, a reading of 7 is neutral, with readings lower than 7 indicating that your soil is somewhat acidic, and readings above 7 indicating that your soil is somewhat alkaline. Since most vegetables, perennials, and roses thrive in slightly acidic soil, a pH reading of about 6.5 is recommended. Your soil test results can be interpreted by your local county extension agent, who will instruct you in adjusting the pH. In general, the addition of lime will raise the pH of acidic soils and elemental sulfur used as an amendment at recommended rates will lower the pH of neutral soils.

Whether your soil is clay, loamy, or sandy, adding organic matter in the form of compost, rotted manure, Milorganite, shredded leaves, or peat moss will improve the capacity of the soil to hold moisture. These organic amendments will also give your soil better drainage and aeration. Organic matter, called humus, acts like a sponge: it holds water, nutrients, and oxygen, and then releases them as the soil dries. All plants, but especially roses, grow better in a soil rich in organic matter and benefit from an application of about 2 inches (5cm) of humus each year—this can be done in any season, whenever you have time. Building your soil is worth the effort. Plants establish more quickly, and digging in your garden is less laborious if you turn in some humus each year.

PLANTING ROSES

In this section you will find all the basics on handling and planting both bareroot and container roses. The optimum time to plant bareroot rose bushes is either spring or autumn, while the plants are dormant, and although most

Plant bareroot rosebushes while they are dormant, in spring or autumn. Form a mound of soil in the bottom of the planting hole and spread the roots out on it; then set plants with the knuckle, or graft union, at soil level (2 to 3 inches [5 to 7.5cm] below soil level in regions where winters are severe).

growers ship in spring, a few offer their stock in the autumn. Either way, the rose grower will ship plants at the appropriate time for planting in your area. Remember to order early: in summer for autumn planting; in autumn for spring planting.

Container-grown roses can be planted at any time during the growing season. These potted roses are commonly available in spring from local nurseries, but sometimes you can also get them in summer and autumn. Be sure the rosebushes have healthy green foliage; avoid weak or ailing bushes discounted as bargains.

Roses are most often sold as dormant bareroot bushes or in containers. If you order bareroot roses through the mail, take a few minutes to care for them when they arrive. Open the carton, mist the roses with a spray of water, close the carton again, and store it in a cool place until you are ready to plant the bush. Bareroot roses can be held for about a week in the carton; if you need to hold them longer, it is a good idea to heel them in, that is, plant the bushes temporarily in the garden, where the roots are in contact with soil.

GUIDE TO BUYING ROSES

Most rosebushes sold are two-year-old, field-grown, grafted plants. Whether they are later purchased as bareroot, packaged, or container plants, the bushes are propagated identically.

Budded roses are two-part plants made up of a strong rose rootstock on the bottom and a flowering cultivar on top. A bud of the flowering cultivar is implanted on the vigorous rootstock by a special grafting technique known as budding. The junction of bud and rootstock is called the bud union. Once joined, the rootstock lends its hardiness and vigor to the flowering cultivar, which quickly grows into a stocky, salable plant. Many roses that tend to perform poorly and lack winter hardiness on their own roots, particularly hybrid teas, are strengthened by this process. In their second autumn in the field, the grafted rosebushes are harvested, machine-pruned, sorted, graded, and refrigerated to keep them fresh for shipping.

Before purchasing roses for your garden, you should take a moment to learn about grading. This will help you to select premium bushes and avoid the temptation to buy discounted seconds. The Association of American Nurserymen has set standards that grade rosebushes into three sizes: No. 1, No. 1½, and No. 2. Grade is a measure of quality. Premium No. 1 grade bushes must have three or four stout canes branched 3 inches (7.5cm) above the bud union, or crown, and a bushy, well-branched root system. Most retail rosebushes sold as bareroot, packaged, or containerized bushes are premium No. 1 grade.

Sometimes the grower runs out of No. 1 grade of a particular cultivar, however, and will ask you to accept No. 1½ grade bushes at a reduced price. These lower-grade bushes typically have only two strong canes or two or three smaller canes, but if treated properly, they will catch up with their more robust siblings in one or two growing seasons.

Avoid No. 2 grade rosebushes altogether. These are bushes from the bottom of the barrel; they have only one cane and are usually packaged as discount roses from cheap mail-order houses. Be wary when you see roses and other shrubs offered at discounted prices far below the retail list prices of reputable nurseries. Read the fine print, notice the grade of rose being offered, and avoid dealing with cheap mail-order houses. There are plenty of reputable rose dealers selling through mail order.

Ordering Roses Through the Mail

The greatest selection of both modern and antique rose cultivars is offered by mail order. In fact, many species roses, old roses, and miniatures are only available through specialty rose nurseries. The beautiful color photographs of rose blooms in catalogs are useful when you're trying to choose roses; however, it is important to read the descriptions and not be lured simply by the glossy pictures. Plant descriptions in catalogs do more than sell rosebushes; they also aid consumers in selecting cultivars suitable for their needs. Information worth gleaning from nursery catalogs includes the mature height and width of bushes, flower size, fragrance, hips, and season of bloom. Also look for valuable data on disease resistance, hardiness, planting distances, and recommended landscape uses.

Buying Container Roses

Rosebushes actively growing in containers are the best choice for novice gardeners. For container plants, premium No. 1 grade bareroot roses are potted up and forced into active growth in greenhouses during the winter. Then in the spring, local nurseries display these rosebushes as container stock. They are in full leaf and typically in bud and bloom when purchased. The advantage of container roses is that they can be planted at any time during the remainder of the growing season, making roses more available to the home gardener. In addition, you can see the color and smell the fragrance of rose blooms instead of making choices from the remote but glossy pages of catalogs.

The available selection of container roses is greater than packaged roses and is continually expanding to meet consumer demand. Large garden centers stock a wide assortment of modern cultivars and also carry some antique roses that have become popular with gardeners. A disadvantage of container roses is that they are more expensive—often nearly double the price of bareroot bushes—because the nursery or grower has done the work of getting the plants into active growth for the consumer.

Select bushes with three or four strong canes and vigorous lateral, or side, branches with clean, healthy, dark green foliage. Avoid plants with broken, damaged, and wilted canes and yellow or diseased foliage. After purchasing, treat your rosebush like any other container plant. Check the soil moisture at least once a day, and water as needed until you can plant it. This care is essential because wilting can cause permanent damage to woody plants such as roses. For the beginner, container roses offer the advantage of personal selection from a local garden center, fail-safe handling of potted bushes, and a longer planting season.

ABOVE: *Rose nursery fields in Hertfordshire, England.*

Container-grown roses are the best choice for novice rose gardeners because they are easy to handle and can be planted at any time during the growing season.
❀

Bareroot bushes tend to dry out on their long journey from harvest to cold storage to you, so when you are ready to plant them, soak them in a bucket of water overnight, or at least for several hours. Take care that bareroot bushes are not exposed to drying winds and sun when you are planting; keep the roots submerged in water or wrapped in wet burlap while you dig the planting holes. For the healthiest-looking plants, prune canes back about half to two thirds their length before planting. This way, the bushes put energy into getting roots established and producing vigorous new canes.

To give your rosebushes a good start, amend the soil with organic matter before planting. Dig planting holes about 2 feet (61cm) wide and 18 inches (46cm) deep. Put a few shovelsful of compost into the planting hole and add back some soil, forming a small mound of soil in the hole on which to spread the roots. Set the bud union, or knuckle, at soil level or an inch or two (2.5 to 5cm) below soil level. Deep planting protects tender roses from frost and also allows the variety to establish its own root system and not be so dependent on its understock. Fill in soil around the roots so that the plant stands up, then water the bush thoroughly, allowing water to fill in air pockets. Backfill soil to the top of the hole and water again. Mound soil up around the canes to prevent drying of dormant canes. When they leaf out in about a month, remove the soil mounds with a stream of water. If you are planting in autumn, leave the soil mound in place until spring. Do not fertilize until first bloom.

Container roses are usually available in midspring and can be planted in any season, providing the ground is not frozen. Make sure to keep container roses well watered before planting. Dig and prepare planting holes just as you would for bareroot roses, taking care that the planting hole is big enough to accommodate the container bush. Give the rosebush plenty of room and avoid crowding the roots into a small planting hole. Always remove rosebushes from the container before planting, even if the container is designed to disintegrate eventually. If left in the container, the roots may fail to push through the cardboard fiber into the surroundng soil, and the bush will die. Plant the rose at the same level it was in the container. Fill in soil around the root ball and water well; when you finish filling in soil, firm it around the plant and make a saucer of soil around the bush so that the water does not run off. Lightly fertilize container-grown roses to help them get established in your garden. After planting, mulch the bushes with shredded leaves, wood chips, or pine needles to retain soil moisture.

TRANSPLANTING ROSEBUSHES

It is always best to move established rosebushes in late autumn or early spring. At these times the bushes are dormant and not subject to wilting. Before digging up the bushes, you can cut back everblooming types such as floribunda and miniature roses, which will make it easier to remove the bush. Tie canes of species and old roses so that you can dig around them comfortably; some pruning may be required on ramblers and climbers to facilitate the move. Carefully dig a trench around the bush with a radius of about 1 foot (30cm) out from the crown. Gently pop the bush out of the hole using a digging fork. Prune off stubs of old canes and broken roots. It's always a good idea to soak the roots in a bucket of water; if the root ball is too big to fit into a bucket, at least cover the roots with a tarp or wet burlap to prevent drying. Replant the bushes, following the instructions for planting a bareroot bush.

PLANTING CLIMBERS AND RAMBLERS TO GROW INTO TREES

If you have a medium-size tree with small leaves, such as a crab apple, cherry, purple plum, or dog-wood, it is a simple task to train a care-free climber or rambler to scramble into the tree. Plant the rose about 3 feet (1m) from the trunk and as the canes grow, guide them along bamboo stakes set at an angle into the crotch of the tree. Once the rose canes reach the first crotch of the tree they'll pull themselves up by their prickles and grow toward the light.

PRUNING

With all garden plants, but especially with roses, the gardener must take charge. Roses are vigorous shrubs, and are kept in bounds and in good health with annual pruning. Removing the oldest canes every year encourages the production of vigorous young ones. Remember that it's always better to prune vigorous roses than not to prune them. Don't be afraid of damaging the bushes. Because their flowers are carried on new wood, prune everblooming and

Prune modern bush roses in late winter or early spring. Remove dead, broken, winter-injured, and crowded canes with a sharp pruning saw, making the cuts flush with the crown.

repeat-blooming roses (such as the miniature 'Gourmet Popcorn'; the polyantha 'The Fairy'; the groundcover 'Scarlet Meidiland'; the shrub rose 'Carefree Wonder'; and the hybrid rugosa 'Hansa') while they are dormant in late winter or early spring. Once-blooming roses (such as the alba 'Konigin von Danemark'; the gallica 'Apothecary's Rose'; the moss rose 'Nuits de Young'; and the damask 'Celsiana'), on the other hand, should be pruned in early summer after their flowers fade because their bloom is carried on canes formed over the summer.

Pruning techniques are the same for all everblooming and repeat-blooming roses. Start by assembling your tools: leather gloves, sharp scissors-type pruners, and a small saw. Remove any dead canes as well as those damaged by winter injury, borers, or from rubbing by neighboring canes. You'll

recognize the damaged canes because they'll appear blackened, often sunken, and dried out. Cut them back to a lateral branch or to clean, healthy wood below the damaged area. Using sharp hand pruners, make clean cuts about ¼ inch (6mm) above an outward-facing bud and slanted slightly away from it. If a cane is dead to the base, remove it at the base by making a clean flush cut with hand pruners or a sharp saw.

Prune the bush to an open vase-shaped form made up of several strong canes. Select the best canes to support the season's flower display: stout, healthy one- or two-year-old canes are the best scaffolding for your flowers. The bark of young healthy canes appears smooth and green or, on deeply colored varieties, slighty reddish. The pith, or center, of the cane is white and crisp.

Pruning Everblooming Modern Bush Roses

Everblooming modern roses benefit from severe pruning in late winter or early spring, which encourages vigorous new growth. For hybrid tea and floribunda roses, prune out dead and damaged canes, leaving three to six healthy canes spaced in an open vase shape. Next, cut the remaining canes back to clean wood, leaving about 6 to 10 inches (15 to 25cm). Prune to outward-facing buds, making cuts about ¼ inch (6mm) above the bud. Make sure to clean up and destroy any cut canes and old leaves, which can harbor overwintering diseases and pests.

Miniatures and polyanthas require a slightly different treatment. Prune the canes of these rosebushes back to about 3 to 6 inches (7.5 to 15cm) and remove all twiggy growth, especially from the center of the bush.

When pruning repeat-flowering roses, remove any deadwood and about one third of the older canes. Reduce the remaining canes by about one third to one half their length.

Pruning and Training Climbers

For the first three years, exercise patience and simply allow climbers to get established. Tie the young canes to their support using jute or plastic snap ties, and deadhead spent blooms to encourage repeat-flowering. Train climbers horizontally or fan the canes out for the best flower production, and remember, they thrive on neglect.

OPPOSITE: Prune vigorous, once-blooming climbers like 'Talisman' in summer, after the flowering period, to remove crowded canes. Don't deadhead spent blooms if you want the rose to set hips. Tie in new canes throughout the summer and tidy wild laterals in late winter.

Once the rose covers its support or fills the allowable space, annual pruning and training are required to maintain it; if you don't cut climbers back regularly, they'll run rampant, turning into true thugs. Prune the roses in late winter while plants are dormant, removing the ties and cutting out dead, broken, and crowded canes, sacrificing older canes in favor of younger ones. Choose healthy, stocky canes to fit the space, tie the chosen ones to their support, and shorten all laterals to about 6 inches (15cm). Deadhead spent blooms throughout the growing season and tie in new canes as they grow.

With vigorous once-blooming climbers, split the pruning chores between summer and late winter. Once bloom begins, don't deadhead if you want hips to form in late summer and autumn. Remove some crowded canes in the summer after blooming and tie in new canes. Then, in late winter, tidy the plants by removing dead and broken canes and reducing wild laterals.

Pruning and Training Ramblers

The long flexible canes of ramblers are best treated as biennials because new canes are produced each season from the crown. Prune canes in summer after flowering and reduce laterals to two or three buds. The vigorous new canes will bear next season's floral display. Tie the young canes to their support with jute or plastic snap ties. The flexible canes can be trained to drape an arch or a split-rail fence; they can also be wrapped around pillars, fanned out on

OPPOSITE: *Even climbing roses must be trained to clamber; tie canes to a sturdy support as they grow. Once established, climbers require annual pruning to keep them in bounds.*

trellises or walls, or trained into trees. Always leave enough canes to fill the space given to the rambler. Once established, roses that grow into trees or cover buildings are best left to fend for themselves. Occasionally, you may need to prune out a dead cane, but otherwise, no care is required.

Pruning Species Roses

Species roses, which typically have an attractive upright vase-shaped habit, are best left to grow naturally, unless they are being trained as wall shrubs or climbers. Some—such as *Rosa roxburghii* and *R. hugonis*—become quite wide, and you can conserve space by removing the lowest canes, which naturally form a sort of skirt. Pruning these canes also creates an ideal spot for an underplanting of bulbs and shade-loving plants. Periodically remove the oldest canes to allow room for young ones, and thin out crowded canes. Also cut back the suckers of suckering shrubs such as *R. rugosa*, *R. nitida*, and *R. palustris*. No other care is required.

Pruning Once-Blooming Old Roses

Once-blooming heirloom roses, including gallica, damask, alba, centifolia, and moss, should be pruned after the flowers have faded in the summer. Thin out crowded canes and shape the bushes by cutting back the stems that carried flowers by two thirds their length. In the spring neaten the bushes by removing dead and broken canes, wild shoots, and dead tips.

CONTROLLING PEST AND DISEASE PROBLEMS

The best defense against pests and diseases is selecting disease-resistant, hardy roses for your garden and practicing good culture. Treat your roses like prize tomatoes: give them a good start by planting them in a sunny location in well-drained soil rich in humus. Keep them watered during dry spells and add compost or well-rotted manure to the soil surface annually.

Monitor plants for damage from pests; if damage is slight, you may choose to live with the tiny holes and blemishes caused by feeding insects but if it is severe, you'll probably want to take action. There are many nontoxic products on the market—including insecticidal soap, neem oil, garden sul-

OPPOSITE: *Grown as wall-huggers, roses with long canes are fanned out and tied to wires or lattice. This rose-covered effect is particularly beautiful on cottages and older houses, as well as on solid walls of stone or brick.*

fur, and horticultural oil—that do no harm to the environment, wildlife, or the gardener. Applications of neem oil or insecticidal soap will effectively control most rose pests. Neem oil, extracted from the Indian neem tree, is an insect growth regulator that prevents larvae from developing into adults; it is also an effective repellant for adult insects such as Japanese beetles, thrips, aphids, rose slugs, and sawflies. Insecticidal soap is a useful miticide and also controls other soft-bodied insects.

If blackspot—a fungal disease common in roses—develops in wet weather, apply sulfur as a fungicide. You can purchase garden sulfur from a garden center; follow the directions on the label for application. Combining sulfur with an antidesiccant or polymer, which acts as a surfactant to spread and hold the fungicide to the leaf surface, improves and extends its effectiveness. For best results, protect the foliage of blackspot-susceptible roses as soon as leaves emerge in spring and repeat the applications as needed.

FERTILIZERS

Roses benefit from the application of a complete or balanced fertilizer annually in early spring. You can use either a homemade organic fertilizer formulated with nutrient-rich materials such as alfalfa meal, fish meal, bonemeal, and gypsum or a commercially prepared granular formulation with organic components. Organic fertilizers clearly state these and other natural ingredients on the label.

Spread fertilizer around each bush and scratch it into the soil. For best results, follow the directions on the label. Repeat-blooming roses benefit from a second fertilization in early summer, which will encourage them to continue blooming. You can apply liquid fertilizers, such as seaweed extract or fish emulsion mixed in water, on a monthly basis. Manure and alfalfa teas also make excellent liquid fertilizers.

HOMEMADE FERTILIZER

It's easy to make your own chemical-free fertilizer. Mix the ingredients together in a large bucket and spread the entire contents around a large rosebush. Use less for smaller bushes and multiply the recipe accordingly if you have several bushes. For maximum growth, fertilize your roses in early spring.

INGREDIENTS
I cup alfalfa meal
I cup fish meal
I cup greensand
½ cup bone meal
I cup gypsum

PROPAGATING ROSES

Enjoy the thrill of making more roses for your garden by learning some simple tips on propagation. There are three types of propagation easily practiced by the home gardener: layering, cuttings, and seed. Growing roses by layering or from cuttings are methods of vegetative propagation or cloning. They produce a plant identical to the parent. Another way to propagate roses is from seed. It's fun and easy to collect the hips of species roses, extract the seeds, and grow them in your home garden. The seedlings will exhibit minor differences from the parent and from each other. Therefore, if you want an exact replica, or clone, of your rose, take cuttings or use the layering technique.

You can easily create more roses at home with a propagation method called layering. Groundcover roses and roses with long, arching canes—such as these ramblers—are perfect for layering.
✿

Layering

Layering is the simplest method of propagation for the home gardener because no special equipment is required. Many species roses, such as *Rosa rugosa*, *R. nitida*, and *R. palustris*, produce underground runners. The part of the runner in contact with the soil usually forms independent roots. Groundcover roses usually root where their stems touch the soil. These stems can easily be dug up, cut from the main shrub, and grown as individuals. These rooted stems are known as layers.

Any rose with an arching, spreading habit can be encouraged to layer. Gently bend over a cane of a shrub you want to layer. Strip off the leaves of the section of the stem to be layered, bury it about 3 inches (7.5cm) deep in the soil with the tip sticking

up, and secure it with a metal stake. If you find that the stem is difficult to root, nick it and apply some rooting hormone before burying it in the soil. Water well and keep the layer moist and covered with soil. Most layers started in the spring will root by mid- to late summer. Tug gently at the buried stem to see whether the layer has rooted. When the layer has formed roots dig it up, cut it from the parent, and plant it in its permanent location or pot it up and give it to a friend. Try layering to increase your collection of old roses, species roses, groundcovers, and shrubs.

Roses from Cuttings

Most modern roses root easily from cuttings taken at any time during the growing season. Species and old roses root best during their bloom period, so be sure to take your cuttings then. Start your cuttings during the first bloom period in late spring or early summer so that they have all summer to grow into new plants. Cuttings root more rapidly in a humid environment, but this does not mean that you need a greenhouse. You can create an adequately humid environment using materials commonly found in the home, such as clear plastic bags and plastic gallon jugs. For cutting propagation you will also need a well-drained soilless rooting medium, rooting hormone, clean plastic pots, sharp hand shears, labels, wire or wire hangers, and a pencil.

Cuttings root best in a sterile, extremely well-drained mix. You can make your own soilless medium by combining three parts perlite to one part peat moss. Do not include soil or compost because they contain organisms that can transmit diseases to the cuttings. Also, soil and compost don't drain well and can cause the cuttings to rot. You can also make your own rooting solution from willow twigs cut into 1-inch (2.5cm) pieces and soaked in a small amount of water for twenty-four hours. Willows contain a natural plant hormone that encourages rooting. If you are reusing plastic pots, be sure to first disinfect them in a 10 percent solution of bleach.

Take cuttings in the early morning. Choose stems that have an open or spent bloom and at least four sets of leaflets; with a sharp pair of hand shears, cut a piece of the stem about 5 to 6 inches (12 to 15cm) long. Separate these cuttings by variety, place them temporarily in plastic bags with moist paper towels, and label the bag clearly with the variety name. The cuttings can be refrigerated for a few hours until you are ready to stick them in the soilless mix.

Prepare your propagation area indoors or in a shaded location in the garden. First, gather together all the materials you will need, including the soilless medium, a disinfected bucket, clean plastic pots, a pencil, wire or wire hangers, plastic bags and ties, and the cuttings. Wet the soilless medium in the bucket by sprinkling it with water and mixing until it is evenly moist, but not soggy. Fill the plastic pots with the moist rooting medium, firm gently with your fingers, and water well. Let the pots drain while preparing the cuttings.

To prepare the cuttings, pinch off the bloom and strip off the two sets of bottom leaflets, leaving two sets of upper leaflets. Trim the leaves in half with a pair of sharp pruning shears. Recut the bottom of the stem on an angle, dip it in water, and then dip it in rooting hormone. If you are using willow water as a rooting hormone, it is best to let the cuttings soak in it for a while.

Miniature roses are the easiest to propagate, so consider experimenting with a miniature cultivar, such as this 'Pretty Polly' rose.

With the pencil, make a depression in the soilless medium and stick each cutting in about 2 inches (5cm) deep so that the bottom two leaf nodes are buried. Small pots hold one cutting each; larger pots will accommodate two or three cuttings of the same variety. Firm the medium around the cuttings and stick a label in the pot. Bend a section of wire or wire hanger into an arch and wedge each end against the sides of the pot to form a dome. Cover the whole thing with a plastic bag and secure it with a plastic tie, creating a tent. Keep cuttings outdoors in a cool, shaded spot where they will receive indirect light. If you don't have access to a yard, keep the cuttings in indirect light on a patio or indoors on a windowsill. Don't expose the pots to direct sunlight because too much heat will build up

HYBRIDIZING YOUR OWN ROSES

Once you've become familiar with rose varieties and their special characteristics of flower color, size, fragrance, and habit, you may want to cross two of your favorite varieties to create a new one. Hybridizing roses is an adventure many gardeners will not want to miss.

Rose flowers are unisexual, that is, they contain both male and female reproductive parts in the same flower. To cross two rose varieties through artificial pollination, first select a rose variety to be the seed, or female, parent. Choose a variety that is fertile, one that produces rose hips. Just as the flowers unfold, remove the petals, then carefully detach the stamens with a small scissors or tweezers. This operation prevents flowers from self-pollinating. Place paper bags over the female flowers to prevent pollination from insects or wind. In about twenty-four hours, remove the bags and inspect the pistils. When they appear slightly sticky they are ready to receive pollen.

Select a rose variety to be the male parent. Just as the flowers unfold, remove the petals. Then remove the stamens with a small scissors or tweezers and place them in a petri dish to ripen. In about twenty-four hours they shed a fine yellow dust. Lightly brush the pollen onto the pistils of the female flowers with a soft brush. Or take a fully open flower that contains yellow pollen dust and brush it directly onto the pistils of receptive female flowers. Replace the paper bags over the female flowers and leave in place for a week or two.

Remove the bags and examine the receptacles, or hips. If a successful cross has been made, the receptacles swell and begin to look like small green hips. In unsuccessful attempts the receptacle dries up and falls off. Allow the hips to ripen and collect them in the autumn. Cut the hips open and check the color of the seeds; mature seeds appear brown, while immature seeds are still white. Care for the seeds just as you would if you were growing roses from any homegrown seed.

Once the roses flower, observe and evaluate the plants. If any exhibit characteristics that interest you, take cuttings and share them with your friends.

---

inside the plastic tent and cause the cuttings to burn. Condensation inside the humid environment of the plastic tents lets you know that the rooting medium is moist. Keep the bags closed unless the condensation clears up and the medium appears dry. If this happens, open the bags, water the cuttings well, drain, and close the bags again.

The cuttings should root in about four weeks. When the new leaves are fully expanded, begin to acclimate the plants to the outdoor temperature. First, poke some holes in the plastic bag; after about

The colorful hips of rugosa rose ripen in late summer and autumn. Once mature, the hips can be collected as a source of seeds.

a week, you can remove the bag altogether. Plant the rooted cuttings in a protected, shaded bed in your garden or pot them up into larger containers in potting soil, and grow them for a few months. Place the pots in filtered light and keep them well watered. Fertilize with a half-strength solution of liquid fertilizer monthly. Plant the young bushes in the garden in the autumn, or overwinter them by sinking the pots in loosened soil and mounding shredded leaves up around the stems.

PROPAGATING BY SEED

To start roses from homegrown seeds, collect hips from species roses in the autumn, when they're a ripe red or orange. You can judge ripeness by cutting the hip open and checking the color of the seeds; mature seeds appear brown, while immature seeds are still white. Remove the mature seeds from the rose hip. Mix one part seed with four parts moist perlite, put the mixture into a plastic bag, seal it, label it with the date, and place it in the refrigerator for three to four months. Make sure to use regular clear plastic bags rather than freezer bags because freezer bags do not allow gas exchange. Refrigerating the seeds this way is known as cold stratification, and mimics the effects of winter.

In early spring plant the seeds indoors in seed flats. Fill a shallow potting tray that has drainage holes with sterile, slightly moist, soilless medium. Sow the seeds by spreading the perlite and seed mixture over the medium. Sprinkle some more of the soilless medium over the seed mixture, and water well. Cover the tray with clear plastic or glass and place it in a bright window, though not in direct sunlight. Seedlings should begin to emerge within a few weeks.

TOP: *Any of the species roses, such as this Moyes rose (Rosa moyesii), can be propagated by seed.*

❁

BOTTOM: *Red-leaved rose (Rosa glauca) boasts fruits that ripen to mahogany red in late summer, when they can be harvested for seed.*

❁

When the seedlings have two sets of true leaves, carefully pick them out of the soilless medium and pot them up into individual containers filled with potting soil. Monitor seedlings closely, as they are extremely delicate and sensitive to wilting from too much direct sun and lack of moisture. After all danger of frost has passed, move seedlings outdoors into a protected, shaded location and continue growing them in the containers. Keep the plants well watered and apply a half-strength solution of liquid organic fertilizer monthly. Allow the seedlings to size up all summer, and plant young roses out in the garden in the autumn.

CHAPTER THREE

DESIGNING WITH ROSES

Climbing roses grace a rustic wood fence—the garlands of flowers provide an effective and ornamental screen.

Roses are a welcome addition to every landscape, and they contribute a romance and elegance to the garden that are unmatched among ornamental plants. With the vast array of easy-care roses available today, there is sure to be one that is perfect for your garden situation. Use climbing roses to decorate arbors, trellises, and walls; train ramblers to grow into trees; plant roses as hedges or groundcovers; and mix them into your flower beds, borders, and herb garden. Even if you have a minimum of space and time, you can enjoy pots of colorful miniature roses on your patio, deck, or terrace. Explore in the following pages the multitude of ways you can enhance your yard with the beauty of roses.

BASIC DESIGN PRINCIPLES

While garden style is largely a matter of individual taste, there are certain design considerations that will affect the way your garden plan evolves. Choosing structures, layouts, and roses that fit your style, siting these elements properly, and planning for year-round enjoyment will help you enjoy your own private Eden for years to come.

Site Analysis

Before you plant a rose, or any other plant, get to know your yard: study the existing plantings, specimen trees, sun and shade patterns, soil composition, and overall style. You might begin by making a rough sketch of the area, including any specimen trees, beds, walkways, and structures such as the house, an arbor, or a gazebo. Once you've examined your sketch, you may find lots of opportunities to incorporate roses into your present design scheme: perhaps you'd like to add a climber to adorn a split-rail fence, a hedge of rugosa roses to provide a colorful screen, shrub roses to a mixed border, and pots of miniatures to decorate a deck or patio.

Remember that roses are sun lovers, and site them accordingly. Estimate the amount of sunlight you receive by observing your yard in summer. An ideal location for roses receives sun from morning through early afternoon, with shade in the heat of midafternoon. If your yard is shaded by deciduous trees and receives lots of dappled light, it's worth taking a chance on roses that tolerate light shade. Try growing species, albas, and hybrid musks in the high shade of deciduous trees similar to the edge of a woodland. You can also train a rambler or *Rosa wichuraiana* climber to grow into one of your trees and let it make its way to the sun.

You'll also want to view your site critically, and get rid of plants that don't fit your vision of the garden. Don't be afraid to change your yard; be ruthless in removing plants that have outgrown their space or serve no structural or ornamental purpose. Once you've performed this elementary assessment and cleanup, you're ready to begin planning for your roses in earnest.

A bed of 'Shreveport' roses, set against a background of sculpted topiary, enhances this formal garden scene with bright, everblooming flowers.

Garden Style

Many factors influence garden style, including the architecture of the house and other structures, existing foundation plantings, and the layout of the garden, driveway, and paths. Style can be generally categorized as either formal or informal. For example, a Georgian-style stone house with a formal entrance walk may cry out for a series of parterres or terrace gardens, while a farmhouse yard may be the perfect setting for a country garden, complete with a meadow planting, kitchen garden, and cottage garden.

A marriage of casual and orderly styles is also possible. Gardens may be formal in outline but informal in treatment, featuring traditional, well-defined beds filled with a riot of flowers. Garden style is dictated by both taste and fashion, and in the end, the decision is yours to make.

The last roses of summer bloom in an early snow. Planting roses that repeat their bloom in late summer and autumn and including those that offer showy hips lets you enjoy your garden all through the year.

Seasonal Variation

One of the most important elements to consider when designing a garden is seasonal variation. Flowering combinations for spring and early summer are easy to manage, and most gardens look great early in the growing season, but don't forget to include plants for autumn and winter interest. The flowers of witch hazel, which appear in late autumn and winter; dramatically colored autumn foliage; peeling bark on specimen trees such as Korean stewartia; the romantic silhouettes of evergreens; autumn and winter berries, especially hollies; and foliage and seedheads on plants such as ornamental grasses all add winter interest to the garden. Plan for each time of year and allow the season's characteristic plants to make their unique contributions to the structure, form, texture, and color of the garden.

Structure

A garden's structure is in large part determined by the trees and shrubs that are its bones. Woody plants create privacy and shade, and divide the garden into separate areas, or "rooms." These garden rooms can be quite naturalistic or may be more formal, depending on the style you've chosen for your garden's design. Hedges, screens, and groupings of shrubs or trees are all strong structural elements, and provide a good framework for other plants. The rose, a woody plant, can play an important part in the shrub layer of a mixed border, providing a substantial background for herbaceous companions.

Interplay of Form and Color

Although gardeners often choose plants for the color and form of their flowers, it is important to integrate into your plans the shape and texture of their foliage as well. In addition, the "habit" of the plant—whether weeping or bushy or fountainlike—should be taken into account. Make sure that you'll appreciate the plant's contribution to the garden even when it is not in flower.

Judgments on superior colors and forms of plants are largely a matter of taste, and what appeals to you will not necessarily catch the eye of another gardener. There are, however, a few basic principles to guide you in combining color, texture, and form.

Remember that the best combinations are often simple and derived from nature. Mixing exotics with native plants or combining too many brightly colored flower cultivars or plants with variegated leaves can result in a garden that looks studied and somehow unnatural. A wild prairie is so beautiful because the flowers exist in drifts that are punctuated by waving grasses; this scheme is repeated again and again, encouraging the eye to travel across the field in a panoramic sweep. Likewise, repeating themes and colors in your garden will tie the design together and provide a pleasing unity.

Strong colors such as orange and yellow are glorious in the garden but when they are thrown together with a riot of other colors, the effect can be jarring. To avoid this problem, use plants with silver foliage as a transition between two groupings of strong colors. White and blue flowers also provide rest for the eye between strong colors.

Ornamental grasses and plants with architectural foliage—such as canna, ornamental rhubarb, castor bean, plume poppy, and banana—provide a sculptural element and can create a dramatic effect. Tall grasses make excellent backdrops in a mixed border, and can act as a screen or hedge as well.

Visit public and private gardens to learn the styles and plant combinations that appeal to you. Study as well the "gardens" in nature: woodlands, meadows, hillsides, and wetlands. These sources, coupled with your own ideas about pleasing colors and plant forms, will help you design your perfect garden.

A formal knot garden of fine-textured, silvery herb foliage plays dramatically against a bright hedge of roses in full bloom.

❀

ABOVE, FROM LEFT TO RIGHT: *'Rose de Rescht', 'Hansa', and 'Dainty Bess'.*
❀

MATCHING ROSES TO YOUR LANDSCAPE NEEDS

Roses bring beauty to your garden and add a touch of elegance to nearly any garden setting. Used appropriately they can also solve landscape problems. For instance, they can be planted on sunny slopes as low-maintenance groundcovers, arranged to create colorful hedges and screens, or used as foundation plantings. Roses with long canes provide vertical accents, and the aristocratic shrubs give architectural form to the mixed border. In a shrub layer in the perennial border, rose blooms give a heady fragrance and a wonderful feeling of lush profusion. All of the smaller types make excellent container specimens to decorate patios and decks.

Roses for the Mixed Border

A simple way to begin incorporating roses into your garden is to select a few easy-care shrubs that appeal to you and use them as accents in a sunny mixed border or any established bed in an herb, flower, or kitchen garden. The best combinations are usually simple—plant individual or small groups of shrub roses surrounded by drifts of your favorite perennial flowers and herbs.

Do give some thought to the rose characteristics that match the garden picture you wish to create. Most shrub roses are informal in habit, and their flowers create a blowsy effect; the larger and fuller the flower, the bolder the impact. The classic rugosa hybrids 'Blanc Double de Coubert' and 'Hansa', for example, produce masses of large, many-petaled flowers on sizable bushes with arching habits. These big bushes provide some substance when positioned in the back of the border, and their repeat bloom is a welcome sight in late summer. To fill the back of the border with excellent flower and fruit displays, choose hardy alba roses such as 'Alba Semi-Plena' and 'Celestial', as well as the Asian species roses, golden rose of China (*Rosa hugonis*), chestnut rose (*R. roxburghii*), and 'Geranium' Moyes rose (*R. moyesii* 'Geranium'). These aristocratic shrubs also provide a beautiful green mantle in summer against which perennials, annuals, and repeat-blooming roses are shown to advantage.

Single, or five-petaled, roses—particularly 'Betty Prior' and 'Dainty Bess'—furnish a delicate, airy impression, carrying their flowers like butterflies on upright stems. Fragrant old damask perpetual roses—'Jacques Cartier', 'Four Seasons', and 'Rose de Rescht', for example—are compact shrub roses ideal for small gardens. Positioned in the second or third layer of the border their damask scent and lovely very double flowers can be well appreciated.

Relaxed in habit, old-fashioned 'Stanwell Perpetual' and modern shrubs 'Lavender Dream' and 'Carefree Delight' form tumbling mounds that create a cascading effect in the front or middle layers of the border. Prostrate groundcovers such as 'The Fairy', 'Red Cascade', and 'Scarlet Meidiland' are studded with clusters of charming tiny flowers, which weave a tapestry of color and texture when mingled with perennials. Blue-flowered perennials such as catmint, salvia, and veronica and the silver foliage of artemisia, lamb's ears, and lavender all make excellent companions for roses.

Foolproof Shrub Roses

If you have given up on roses or are timid because they tend to die in your care, try some of the following foolproof types. Shrub roses 'Blanc Double de Coubert' and 'Frau Dagmar Hartopp' are superior rugosa roses that bloom over a long season with little attention from the gardener. Favored by English garden designer Gertrude Jekyll, aristocratic 'Blanc Double de Coubert' is a superb specimen shrub that integrates well with perennials and herbs. Shapely buds open to large, loosely double flowers that exude intense fragrance. Typical of rugosa hybrids, 'Blanc Double de Coubert' makes a dense, prickly shrub with wrinkled, dark green foliage. The arching to rounded shrubs grow 4 to 4½ feet (1.2 to 1.3m) tall and 4 feet (1.2m) wide.

'Blanc Double de Coubert' is a great rose whose abundant late spring bloom coincides with the lovely blue flowers of false indigo (*Baptisia australis*); these two make a stunning combination in late May. In the autumn this rugosa hybrid contributes characteristic late blooms and golden bronze foliage. The specimen shrub rose should find a home in nearly any sunny border. For a good crop of hips in the autumn, substitute superb *Rosa rugosa* var. *alba*; its pale pink buds open to large, single, fragrant flowers that are excellent repeat-bloomers.

A compact hybrid rugosa, 'Frau Dagmar Hartopp' grows only 3 to 3½ feet (1m) tall and wide and is covered with silver-pink single flowers almost continuously. In a small sunny space create season-long interest by planting 'Frau Dagmar Hartopp' faced with the blue spires of Russian sage and dark blue 'Persimmon' Siberian irises. Autumn flowers and ripe red fruits look beautiful with the russet seedheads of 'Autumn Joy' stonecrop, another tough companion. These combinations all thrive in hot spots along driveways and walks, and in harsh city and seashore sites.

New England shining rose (*R. nitida*)—the smallest of the eastern North American species roses—is another tough shrub. Deep rose-pink single flowers with a light fragrance bloom for several weeks in June, with small red fruits ripening in late summer. When it is cultivated in gardens the low shrub can easily reach 3 feet (1m) in height and 2 feet (61cm) in width from suckering stems. Small, pointed, glossy leaves—handsome throughout the season—color to brilliant red-orange and scarlet in the autumn. New England shining rose is worth growing simply for its striking autumn color. Clean, polished foliage enhances mixed borders all season long and makes this shrub an excellent foil for companion herbaceous plants.

For a striking combination, plant New England shining rose in the front of the border, positioned against elegant red-leaved rose (*R. glauca*), which boasts handsome gray-blue foliage tinged with burgundy. Underplant these roses with star of Persia allium and 'Honorine Jobert' anemone for lush summer foliage and crisp white autumn blooms. New England shining rose is a great choice for a wild garden because it mixes extremely well with wildflowers and thrives under almost any conditions; its dwarf size also recommends its use as a foreground shrub or rock garden specimen.

The majestic hybrid rugosa, 'Blanc Double de Coubert' has long been favored for its pure white flowers and continual bloom.

Antique Roses for Repeat Bloom

Antique roses that offer repeat bloom in late summer and autumn add a unique touch to the garden. Imported from China at the beginning of the nineteenth century, China roses are rarely out of bloom, and they passed the gene for repeat bloom along to our modern roses. China roses produce lots of small flowers that lend an air of sprightly enchantment throughout the season. They can always be counted on to give a bit of color to the autumn garden.

'Mutabilis'—the most disease-resistant of the China roses—produces pointed copper buds that open to dainty, single, apricot-orange flowers. As the blooms age they change from apricot to pink and crimson. Airy bushes reach a height of 3 to 4 feet (1 to 1.2m). 'Mutabilis' always attracts attention because of its elegant five-petaled blossoms, which resemble butterflies. Enhance this rose by combining it with sky blue spikes of 'Souvenir d'André Chaudron' Siberian catmint, which mingle easily with the copper butter-flies of 'Mutabilis'.

An excellent compact Bourbon rose (which, when grown in northeastern gardens, resembles a low-growing floribunda), 'Souvenir de la Malmaison' inherited the China gene for nonstop bloom. Exquisite, blush pink, fragrant flowers cover the bush throughout the season. One of the best of the repeat-blooming old roses for small gardens, this admired shrub grows to only 2 feet (61cm). Its pink flowers are complemented by purple perennial geraniums and lavender.

The unsung heroes of the antique rose world, fragrant damask perpetual roses—including 'Jacques Cartier', 'Rose de Rescht', and 'Four Seasons'—prove to be the easiest and most rewarding of the old roses to cultivate. These shrubs are vigorous, hardy, and disease-resistant.

'Jacques Cartier' is a bushy compact shrub crowned with tight clusters of fat crimson buds that open to very double, silver-pink, fragrant flowers. Its pink flowers are borne on short, bristly stems and are shown to handsome effect when underplanted with silver-foliage perennials.

'Four Seasons' bears damask-scented, light crimson, double blooms on a prickly-stemmed loose shrub. Always at home with old-fashioned herbaceous companions, 'Four Seasons' looks particularly beautiful mixed with foxgloves, poppies, and love-in-a-mist.

The bonus of repeat bloom makes the charming, fragrant flowers of 'Jacques Cartier' a favorite among gardeners.

OPPOSITE: *The everblooming climber 'America' decorates a pergola with its exquisite blooms.*

BELOW: *The roses dubbed "carefree" live up to their names. All 'Carefree' cultivars show excellent disease resistance.*

One of the best and most compact of the damask perpetual roses, 'Rose de Rescht' grows only 3 feet (1m) tall and less wide. Blooms are fuchsia-red and well scented, with many packed petals that fade to purple as they age. It offers its bright flowers on short, bristly stems covered with rough, medium-green leaves. Flowers are produced freely in early summer with liberal repeat bloom in autumn. Underplant the aristocratic 'Rose de Rescht' with 'Bath's Pink' dianthus, or blend it with the lavender globes of star of Persia in spring followed by the dainty autumn blooms of Japanese anemone.

The New Care-Free Shrub Roses

Their names signify freedom from disease: 'Carefree Beauty', 'Carefree Wonder', and 'Carefree Delight'. These are some of the excellent new shrub roses introduced by Conard-Pyle over the past several years. With its large, rose-pink blooms and orange-red autumn hips, 'Carefree Beauty' makes a popular choice for low-maintenance gardens. This hardy bush grows to 5 feet (1.5m) tall and 3 feet (1m) wide. 'Carefree Wonder', a 1992 All-America Rose Selection, forms an upright shrub that grows to 5 feet (1.5m) and bears large, double, deep pink flowers with creamy reverse. Fragrance is very slight but present in the autumn blooms. A winner of the 1996 All-America Rose Selections award, the rounded shrub of 'Carefree Delight' grows to about 3 feet (1m) tall and wide. The bushes are covered with small glossy leaves and large clusters of single, deep pink flowers that bloom almost continuously. The shrubs grow energetically, repeat their bloom, and hold on to most of their foliage. Complement the blooms of these pink roses with sweeps of blue-flowered catmint.

Everblooming Groundcovers

One of the best and most enduring of the low-growing roses is 'The Fairy'. Generously covered in large trusses of small, pink flowers, bushes mound about 2 feet (61cm) high and 3 feet (1m) wide, and are clothed in small, polished leaves. Great spring combinations are easy to create using any of the blue-flowered ornamental herbs such as catmint and salvia; for a sublime autumn display allow pink pompon-shaped flowers of 'The Fairy' to cascade over an underplanting of purple-leaved 'Herrenhausen' ornamental marjoram set against a backdrop of *Amsonia hubrectii* in its golden-russet autumn foliage color. 'The Fairy' also makes an excellent everblooming edging plant for paths.

'Red Cascade', which mounds to a height of about 2 to 3 feet (61cm to 1m) with a spread of 4 feet (1.2m), is another terrific creeper. Use it as a low hedge or edging plant, or allow it to creep over a stone wall. The tiny, bright red flowers of 'Red Cascade' are perfectly complemented by burgundy- and silver-leaved plants in a mixed border.

'Scarlet Meidiland' is a more industrial-type groundcover that will easily spread out to hug about a 6-foot (1.8m) area. It will tumble gracefully down a slope, smothering weeds in its wake.

Climbers and Ramblers

Roses with long canes—climbers, ramblers, and even lax shrubs—bring the dimension of height to the garden, soften hard architectural lines, camouflage unsightly buildings, and bestow a touch of elegance. To add vertical accent to your garden, train climbers or ramblers on trellises or arches; over arbors, garden structures, or walls; or into trees. Unlike some vines, roses do not naturally climb, so canes must be tied to their support with jute or plastic snap ties. Both repeat- and once-blooming roses will share their support amicably with a clematis or honeysuckle vine, enhancing color combinations and extending bloom time. Where vertical space permits, climbers, ramblers, and lax shrubs are shown to advantage trained as espaliers or fence-huggers. Rampant ramblers and large-flowered climbers are typically reserved to fill large spaces or cover any homely spots, including sheds, garages, and dead trees.

Both esteemed and held in awe as the giants of the rose world, roses with long canes live up to their reputation as tough, trouble-free plants. Certainly they prove to be among the easiest and most satisfying roses to grow. With sturdy support and a little training, climbers and ramblers are ready to lend romance to any garden scene.

Roses trained as climbers are a must for the uninitiated or for any gardener looking for an obvious success, because most varieties are simply indestructible. Rambler 'Dorothy Perkins', for instance, widely planted at the turn of the century, is commonly found suckering along roadsides long after the homestead and its inhabitants have vanished. From relatively short climbers such as 'Westerland, 'Dortmund', and 'White Cockade' to massive scramblers including 'Kiftsgate', 'Kew Rambler', and 'Seagull', many superior landscape plants are found among this class of roses.

OPPOSITE: *'Dorothy Perkins', shown clambering over a weathered fence, is one of the great old Rosa wichuraiana ramblers. Introduced in 1901, it's still growing strong.*

Pillar Roses

As an alternative to trellises and espaliers, consider wrapping long canes around freestanding pillars, towers, and obelisks to create charming accents in mixed borders and to conserve space in small gardens. There are many ornamental garden structures that can be used as pillars for roses with long canes. An inexpensive pillar can be constructed by simply sinking a 10- or 12-foot (3 or 3.7m) rot-resistant post

RECOMMENDED LONG-CANED ROSES

The following roses all have long canes that can be trained to grow on a wall, up a trellis, around a pillar, or into a tree. Except where noted, these roses are all hardy in Zones 5 to 9.

• 'Alberic Barbier' produces clusters of yellow buds that open in June to fragrant large, pure white, scented flowers that last for several weeks. Canes stretch 15 feet (4.6m) tall and wide depending on training, and are clothed in glossy foliage that is extremely disease-resistant. This is a great, though underused, rose.

• 'Albertine' is a glorious sight in full bloom: its soft pastel flower color is appreciated in gardens around the world. Apricot-copper buds open to light salmon-pink fragrant flowers that cover the plant for several weeks in June. Canes reach 15 to 18 feet (4.6 to 5.6m) and are covered in disease-free foliage.

• 'Alchymist' is celebrated for its old-fashioned apricot blooms, which are fragrant and produced in abundance for several weeks in early June. The upright, vigorous canes stretch 6 to 8 feet (1.8 to 2.4m) tall and wide. Train a clematis or honeysuckle over the rose canes to extend bloom season and to hide any defoliation from blackspot, to which this rose is somewhat susceptible.

• 'America' is rarely out of bloom. Its salmon hybrid tea–type flowers are scented and produced nearly continuously. Canes stretch 8 to 10 feet (2.4 to 3m) and are easily trained on a pillar. Grow a violet-flowered clematis such as Italian clematis (*Clematis viticella*) over it for a stunning color contrast. 'America' exhibits good disease resistance.

• 'American Pillar', one of the most popular climbers of all time, bears huge clusters of carmine-pink single flowers on canes that stretch 15 to 20 feet (4.6 to 6m). It is resistant to blackspot but does mildew after the bloom. It is still worth growing, especially into a large tree, which will camouflage its marred foliage.

• 'Chevy Chase' is a red rambler that is both vigorous and disease-free. Large clusters of small, crimson flowers attract attention. This is a versatile rose that reaches 12 to 15 feet (3.7 to 4.6m) trained on arches, fences, and into trees. 'Kew Rambler' is a similar variety with trusses of small, single, light pink flowers that look like apple blossoms. Both are disease-free.

• 'City of York' is one of the best white climbers. The scented, semidouble flowers are pure white and produced in huge clusters. Canes clothed in clean foliage reach 10 to 12 feet (3 to 3.7m) tall with a similar spread depending on training. If this rose is deadheaded after the June bloom, it will produce a few late-summer flowers.

• 'Dortmund' features huge clusters of large, five-petaled red flowers branded with a white eye. If you train it as a climber, expect it to stretch 8 to 10 feet (2.4 to 3m); foliage is glossy and typically disease-free. This rose is a knock-out in full bloom and will repeat reliably if deadheaded religiously.

• 'Eden' (also called 'Eden Climber') belongs in every garden where pastel flowers are desired. Fat, creamy buds open to scented double blooms of soft pink swirled with creamy yellow. Deadhead to encourage repeat bloom and grow a clematis over the rose to provide seasonal interest. Heavy canes covered with disease-resistant foliage easily scale a 10-foot (3m) trellis.

2 to 3 feet (61cm to 1m) into the ground. Choose a short climber or lax shrub rose with a height of 8 to 10 feet (2.4 to 3m) to train up the post. Periodically, as the climber grows, wrap the canes around the pillar and tie them into place with jute or plastic snap ties.

Many repeat-blooming modern climbers, such as 'America', 'Dortmund', 'Westerland', and 'White Cockade', make excellent pillar roses. There are also several lax shrubs in the antique rose

• 'Honorine de Brabant' is a Bourbon rose that is worth growing for its fragrant lilac-and-violet-striped flowers and repeat bloom. Wrapped on a pillar, 'Honorine de Brabant' grows to about 6 feet (1.8m); train a clematis over it for extended bloom. Disease resistance is good.

• 'Madame Plantier' is a great rose for the novice. It is a hardy, disease-free alba rose with a lax habit, and will accept some light shade. Buds are tinged crimson but open to pure white, fragrant flowers, which are quartered and have a button center. Trained as a climber, 'Madame Plantier' stretches about 6 feet (1.8m). It looks charming scrambling into a small tree or wrapped on a pillar with a clematis to pick up the bloom after June. (Zones 4 to 8).

• 'New Dawn' is the repeat-blooming sport of the large-flowered climber 'Dr. W. Van Fleet' and bears flowers that are identical to its parent's. Blooms are shell pink, scented, and high-centered in shapely hybrid tea form. Vigorous canes easily reach 12 feet (3.7m) or more with a similar spread and are clothed in glossy, disease-resistant foliage. 'New Dawn' is parent to a host of repeat-blooming modern climbers and remains one of the best of them. No garden should be without it.

• 'Parade' is a 'New Dawn' offspring, and is simply the best climber in its color range. Deep pink, old-fashioned flowers are scented and bloom in profusion in early summer with excellent repeat; in fact, this rose is rarely out of bloom. Disease resistance is also excellent. Expect 'Parade' to stretch 10 feet (3m) with a similar spread.

• 'Seagull' in full bloom is an awe-inspiring sight. This rose produces huge clusters of small, single, pure white blossoms with a sweet scent. Flowers bloom for several weeks in early summer. This disease-free rambler easily stretches 15 feet (4.6m) or more, and is excellent for training into a large crab apple tree.

• 'Westerland' generally blooms from Memorial Day to the 4th of July and then produces scattered bloom through the summer and autumn. The flowers are large, tangerine-orange in color, and exude a fruity fragrance. Canes stretch about 8 feet (2.4m) tall and wide depending on training; foliage is extremely disease-resistant. This rose looks amazing with the annual sweet potato vine 'Blackie' grown over it, and its flowers also contrast beautifully with a red clematis such as scarlet clematis (Clematis texensis).

• 'White Cockade' inherited the noble genes of 'New Dawn'. It is rarely out of bloom and canes are clothed in clean, glossy foliage. Its flowers are pure white with a light scent and a hybrid tea–type form. 'White Cockade' makes an excellent short climber or pillar rose; it grows about 8 feet (2.4m) tall and looks wonderful sharing its support with lavender-blue 'Mrs. Cholmondeley' clematis woven through it for interesting color contrast.

• 'Zéphirine Drouhin' is the most popular of the fragrant Bourbon roses. Its floppy habit and thornless canes make it easy to train as an 8- to 10-foot (2.4 to 3m) climber. Flowers are deep pink, semidouble, and exquisitely perfumed. The main show is in June, but it typically produces a few autumn blooms. It is susceptible to blackspot and typically loses its bottom leaves. Train a clematis over it to extend the bloom season and hide its bare canes later in the season (Zones 6 to 9).

OPPOSITE: 'Albertine' has delightful pale blooms that look lovely twining up a trellis or over an arbor.
ABOVE: The popular rose 'New Dawn' is extremely vigorous, so when growing it as a climber make sure to give it ample support.

'Dortmund' trained on a pillar contributes a charming vertical accent in the corner of a formal garden. The lush, romantic nature of climbing roses helps to soften the severe geometry of formal plantings.

class, including fragrant 'Honorine de Brabant', 'Zéphirine Drouhin', and 'Reine des Violettes', that are beautifully displayed on a pillar. Both 'Zéphirine Drouhin' and 'Reine des Violettes' are thornless, which makes them a joy to train. Weave clematis or honeysuckle through the rose to complement its bloom colors and hide bare canes later in the season.

Climbers as Wall Shrubs

Roses are easily trained up a wall—just attach wires or a lattice onto which the canes can be tied. Fan out the canes or bend them nearly horizontally for maximum bloom. Some of the larger repeat-blooming climbers, such as 'New Dawn', 'Eden', and 'Parade', will quickly cover a wall with seasonal floral displays. These superior varieties stretch effortlessly to 12 feet (3.7m) high and wide, depending on how you train them. Plant these climbers about 8 feet (2.4m) apart and fan the canes to fill the space. 'New Dawn', 'Parade', and 'Eden' are magnificent when grown in combination, for their contrasting shades of pink—from blush to deep pink—blend beautifully. Each produces masses of fragrant, old-fashioned, double blooms, and repeat bloom is respectable. 'Parade' is the most reliable producer of all-season flowers and is rarely out of bloom.

Some of the most fragrant and beautiful roses give their all for several weeks in June and overwhelm with their beauty, then quietly become part of the green background. The fragrant cultivars 'Alchymist', 'Goldbusch', and 'Maigold' bear huge, old-fashioned flowers in shades of apricot or yellow for several weeks in early summer. Trained as wall shrubs, each covers a space about 8 to 10 feet

(2.4 to 3m) high and less wide, depending on training. Don't let their short bloom time deter you from planting these exquisite beauties; simply grow clematis or honeysuckle over the shrubs to extend and enhance color in the garden.

Training Roses to Grow into Trees

Another way to enjoy climbing and rambling roses is to allow them to scramble into trees (see page 45 for planting instructions). To adorn young trees, consider planting the antique 'Madame Plantier', a lax alba rose that stretches about 6 to 7 feet (1.8 to 2m) and provides a profusion of fragrant blooms in early summer. 'Madame Legras St. Germain', a similar pure white rose, also makes an excellent subject for growing into a small tree.

Larger trees require more vigorous ramblers, such as 'Seagull', 'Chevy Chase', 'Kew Rambler', and 'Marie Viaud', all excellent, disease-free cultivars. Each scrambles about 15 feet (4.6m) with agility and then throws its huge clusters of June blooms over the tree limbs. These ramblers attract plenty of attention when their lovely blossoms cascade from the tree, but fade discreetly from view when not in bloom. The fragrant, pure white flowers and red hips of 'Seagull' contrast nicely with purple plum foliage. The rampant climber 'American Pillar' can also be given support in a large tree, which it will scale effortlessly, ultimately stretching about 20 feet (6m). This rose is susceptible to mildew after its bloom—although it is resistant to blackspot—but is worth growing for its massive bloom. Trained into a tree, its host helps to camouflage the marred foliage.

Pink 'May Queen' scrambles into the branches of a small plum tree.

❀

*The sunny flowers of
'Maigold' are sweetly scented.*
❁

The Superheroes: Rosa wichuraiana *Climbers*

Several beautiful and fragrant *Rosa wichuraiana* cultivars easily stretch 15 to 20 feet (4.6 to 6m) and provide impressive flower displays for several weeks in June; large-flowered climbers 'Albéric Barbier', 'Albertine', 'City of York', 'Dr. W. Van Fleet', and 'Silver Moon' reach the second story of a building when trained up. Their parent, *R. wichuraiana*, commonly known as memorial rose, is a prostrate Asian species noted for its garlands of flowers freely given over a long season and its shiny, healthy foliage. Its disease resistance has been passed on to its offspring.

R. wichuraiana climbers are among the most interesting and versatile roses. With training, these superheroes easily scale large trees, effortlessly make their way up over a roof, and plunge recklessly down inhospitable slopes, smothering weeds in their wake. They serve a multiplicity of uses in gardens and although they are typically used as climbers, they also make excellent groundcovers and impenetrable shrub masses.

Hedges, Screens, and Masses

Roses make wonderful informal hedges, masses, screens, and foundation plantings. Use rugged rugosa roses such as *Rosa rugosa* var. *alba* and 'Roseraie de l'Hay', which form dense, bushy masses and hedges. These roses also offer healthy foliage, repeat bloom, hips, and autumn color. Repeat-blooming easy landscape roses 'Carefree Wonder', 'Carefree Delight', and 'William Baffin' are also superior selections for a low-maintenance hedge or mass.

Roses for Light Shade

Although most roses, especially repeat- and everblooming types, thrive on at least a half day of full sun, many once-blooming roses will tolerate the high shade of deciduous trees at the edge of a woodland. The roses get full sun in spring while their flower buds are forming, before trees leaf out, and

receive dappled light throughout the summer. Such a situation is a good spot in which to naturalize species roses such as sweetbriar (*Rosa eglanteria*), and Scotch rose (*R. spinosissima*). Where summers are hot and humid, mountain species such as red-leaved rose (*R. glauca*) and New England shining rose (*R. nitida*) appreciate some afternoon shade. The prostrate species *R. wichuraiana*, along with groundcovers 'Petite Pink' and 'Snow Carpet', also thrives in some light shade. Old roses from the alba group—'Alba Semi-Plena', 'Maxima', and 'Madame Plantier'—accept dappled shade, and their white flowers light up the edge of the woodland. Repeat-blooming roses for light shade include the groundcover 'Scarlet Meidiland' and hybrid musks 'Cornelia' and 'Ballerina'.

Roses for Decks and Patios

Decorate patios and decks with pots of colorful miniature roses—these diminutive beauties are available in nearly every color of the rainbow. Those with a cascading habit such as 'Green Ice', 'Sweet Chariot', and 'Rise 'n' Shine' look beautiful in hanging baskets; for a rose with a bushier habit, try 'Popcorn', 'Sweet Sunblaze', or 'Magic Carrousel'. To create a container garden on a larger scale, choose tubs, barrels, and urns and fill them with floribunda roses such as 'Showbiz', 'Playboy', and 'Sunsprite'; polyantha roses 'The Fairy' and 'Baby Faurax'; and the big climbing miniature 'Red Cascade'.

TOP TO BOTTOM:
'Playboy', 'Sunsprite', and
'Showbiz'.

GREAT GARDEN DESIGNS

OPPOSITE: *'Iceberg' roses contribute mounds of alabaster flowers to the silver and white design of this mixed border.*

Hybrid musk roses infuse this shrub border with glorious scent and color. Whether your garden is classically formal or artlessly casual, it will only be enhanced with a planting of lush and healthy roses.

Gardening with roses is an experience that you won't want to miss. If you love the look of a garden brimming with roses, but fear that your thumb isn't green enough to grow these reputedly difficult flowers, take heart. The roses available to gardeners today are far more versatile than most of us realize. For every situation and every type of garden—whether you live in a hot, dry climate, near the seaside, or in the mountains—there is a rose that will fit your landscape.

This chapter offers fifteen specific plans that will guide you as you begin to garden with easy-care roses. Follow the plans exactly or adapt them to suit your taste and your space. Feel free to mix and match the ideas and plants suggested here, experimenting with different colors, textures, and themes.

As you learn to place plants in dynamic combinations, you may discover a secret longing to create a garden that now lives only in your imagination. Perhaps this garden picture comes from a childhood memory; maybe it's an impression from a visit to a special garden; or perhaps your fantasy garden is derived from the descriptions in a favorite book. Whatever the inspiration for your ideal garden, allow its image in your mind's eye to direct you in choosing flower color and form, selecting foliage patterns, and placing plants. Gardening with roses is an art, and as with any other art, it takes time to develop a sense of which experiments really work and which do not.

The garden plans in this chapter are scaled to small yards, and they employ all types of easy-care roses. Like other flowering shrubs, roses are a gregarious, diverse group that mingle effortlessly with herbaceous flowers and other plants. Here you'll find recommendations for companion perennials, annuals, shrubs, vines, herbs, vegetables, and ornamental grasses, all of which beautifully complement roses even as they enhance your garden with various colors and textures and provide seasonal interest. All designs are for use in Zones 5 to 9 unless otherwise noted. For the coldest regions (Zone 4), substitutions are recommended.

BELOW: *'New Dawn' is the perfect rose for your dooryard garden.*

❀

BOTTOM: *If you'd prefer blooms in a deeper pink, substitute 'Parade' for the 'New Dawn' climber.*

❀

DOORWAY GARDEN:
A Few Cherished Roses to Greet You

Planting a few favorite roses by the door of the house is a tradition that goes back to colonial times. Not only is the dooryard garden simple to plant and easy to maintain, but it is placed precisely where it can be enjoyed most.

Climbing roses are an excellent choice for the doorway, since they can be trained to grow up a sunny wall and over the top of the door. In the early years of the twentieth century an American rose hybridizer, Dr. Walter Van Fleet, created many large-flowered climbers that he called dooryard roses. He envisioned his strain of climbing roses adorning doorways, porches, and picket fences, filling front entrances and side yards with fragrant flowers that welcomed family

and friends home. The best-known of the Van Fleet hybrids, named 'Dr. W. Van Fleet', was one of his last great rose introductions. Often found growing in old gardens, this vigorous, once-blooming climber is still admired for its sprays of long-stemmed, hybrid tea–type flowers, which are blush pink and beautifully scented. Only Mother Nature could have improved upon this exceptional climber, and she did! 'New Dawn', a sport, or mutant, of 'Dr. W. Van Fleet', is an everblooming variety that is a great choice for decorating your doorway.

❀ Design Basics

The doorway garden is a simple design that provides cheerful blossoms from late winter until autumn frost, and even adds some winter beauty to greet family members as they come and go. If your front door is shaded by the house or large foundation plantings, consider planting a rose doorway garden by a sunny patio, terrace, back door, side yard, or garage entrance.

Since roses require support to climb, you'll need to install a sturdy lattice beside the door for the 'New Dawn' climber. Train the rose canes as they grow by tying them to the structure using natural jute or black plastic snap ties. To contrast with the blush-colored flowers of 'New Dawn', plant small-flowered 'Purpurea Plena Elegans' Italian clematis to grow over the 'New Dawn' climber. The clematis will happily throw out trusses of nodding, dusky, maroon-purple rosettes, extending the bloom period for your dooryard garden well into summer. If your site allows room for one special shrub, you might choose 'Carol Mackie' daphne for its heavenly scented flowers and variegated, evergreen leaves. Or consider a special tree peony or another favorite flowering shrub.

Informal drifts of perennials spilling out of the bed add a touch of charm to the doorway garden and complete this simple design. 'Honorine Jobert' Japanese anemones provide crisp white autumn flowers and can be underplanted with daffodils, alliums, or other favorite spring bulbs to provide a succession of bloom. A pleasing tapestry of lavender, mountain cranberry, thyme, and

perennial geranium adds seasonal flowers, fragrant foliage, berries, and evergreen leaves for winter interest. These plants thrive in sharply drained soil; for best results mix pea gravel in the planting hole.

Because your doorway garden will be viewed at close range, attention to detail is important. For example, although many of the recommended plants are evergreen, perennial geranium is deciduous and dies back in winter, leaving its dormant stems behind. Make sure to grow it among clumps of small-leaved evergreen 'Dragon's Blood' stonecrop (*Sedum spurium* 'Dragon's Blood'), which produces attractive burgundy foliage in winter. Tuck in a few clusters of ephemeral, bright yellow spring adonis (*Adonis vernalis*) to brighten the doorway in early spring. For a lush tropical mood in summer, plant a tub with annual angel trumpet (*Datura meteloides*). These huge, pure white, fragrant flowers bloom nonstop, even in hot, humid weather.

❀ Roses for the Doorway Garden

The charming blush pink flowers of 'New Dawn' are shown to advantage against stone, but they also blend well with brick or wood. If you'd prefer a rose with deep pink blossoms, substitute 'Parade', a wonderful 'New Dawn' offspring. For pure white blooms, choose classic 'City of York' or the attractive climbing tea rose 'Sombreuil'.

THE DOORWAY GARDEN
PLANT LIST

1. 'New Dawn' climbing rose (*Rosa* 'New Dawn'); if desired, intertwine 'Purpurea Plena Elegans' Italian clematis (*Clematis viticella* 'Purpurea Plena Elegans')

2. 'Carol Mackie' daphne (*Daphne* × *burkwoodii* 'Carol Mackie')

3. 'Purple Sensation' allium (*Allium aflatunense* 'Purple Sensation') and 'Honorine Jobert' Japanese anemone (*Anemone* × *hybrida* 'Honorine Jobert')

4. 'Provence' lavender (*Lavandula* × *intermedia* 'Provence')

5. Mountain cranberry (*Vaccinium vitis-idaea* var. *minor*)

6. Thyme (*Thymus praecox arcticus* 'Coccineus')

7. Perennial geranium (*Geranium dalmaticum*)

8. Angel trumpet (*Datura meteloides*)

ABOVE, FROM LEFT TO RIGHT: *'Alba Semi-Plena', 'Frau Dagmar Hartopp', rose hips*

❀

OPPOSITE: *Roses have long found a home in the country kitchen garden. Here, a gallica rose mixes happily with golden lemon thyme and the lavender heads of chives.*

❀

KITCHEN GARDEN:
Simple, Edible, and Beautiful

A small plot by the kitchen door provides a delightful place to grow a blend of choice vegetables, herbs, fragrant roses, and flowers. Rose petals can be picked and used fresh as garnishes or dried for use in potpourri. The fruits of the rosebush, which are called hips, have long been valued as a source of vitamin C, and are used to make teas and jellies.

The kitchen garden is designed to be both useful and attractive; it is composed of plants with colorful flowers and fruits, and its texture patterns are highlighted by burgundy-bronze and silver foliage. This garden exudes wonderful fragrances, particularly when its herbs and flowers are gathered, but also when you brush by them or after a light rain.

❀ Design Basics

This design shows the kitchen garden planted beside a wall covered with bright scarlet runner beans and honeysuckle vines, which are trained along wire or lattice. If you don't have a wall, this effect could also be achieved using a fence as support for the vines. Alternatively, a freestanding tripod fabricated from 10-foot (3m) wooden poles makes a rustic truss for vines. Add a few stepping stones for access into the garden, and edge the bed with pavers or flagstones.

Position the shrub rose 'Frau Dagmar Hartopp', or any other you might choose, toward the back of the bed and surround it with richly colored cherry tomatoes, hot peppers, chives, red-stemmed Swiss chard, arugula, and herbs. Rosemary, lavender, fennel, basil, thyme, sage, and oregano are favorites, and the low spreaders fill the foreground and gracefully spill out over the bed. Annual flowers also find a place in the kitchen garden: bright red globe amaranth and multicolored trailing nasturtiums, which bloom all summer, can be directly seeded into the garden following an early season crop of arugula and leaf lettuce.

In addition to fresh edibles, the kitchen garden provides a wealth of plant materials that dry well. Gather rose petals, lavender flowers, globe amaranth, and leaves of scented geraniums to make a delightful potpourri.

Roses for the Kitchen Garden

The rugosa rose 'Frau Dagmar Hartopp' is a perfect choice for the kitchen garden. This compact shrub grows to 3 feet (1m) high and wide, with clean, dark green, wrinkled leaves that repel disease and insects. Flowers are large, with only five petals, and very fragrant. Charming crimson buds open into silver-pink single flowers that are produced almost continuously until late summer, when they are followed by large red hips. Roses that produce hips are valuable because their fruits are an excellent natural source of vitamin C, and can be dried for use in rose hip tea.

Where space permits, one of the fragrant alba roses grown for its attar, such as 'Alba Semi-Plena' or 'Suaveolens', is also a good candidate for the kitchen garden. Each produces pure white, semidouble flowers that open to reveal a center of golden stamens; petals are saturated with essential oils and exude such intense fragrance that they maintain their perfume even when dried. Sprays of the charming white flowers are produced freely for several weeks in late spring on vigorous, lax canes that reach 6 to 7 feet (1.8 to 2m) in height. Both are large shrubs, especially 'Alba Semi-Plena'. Manage their floppy canes by wrapping them on a pillar, growing them as espaliers, or training them to grow into a small tree, thus conserving space in a small garden.

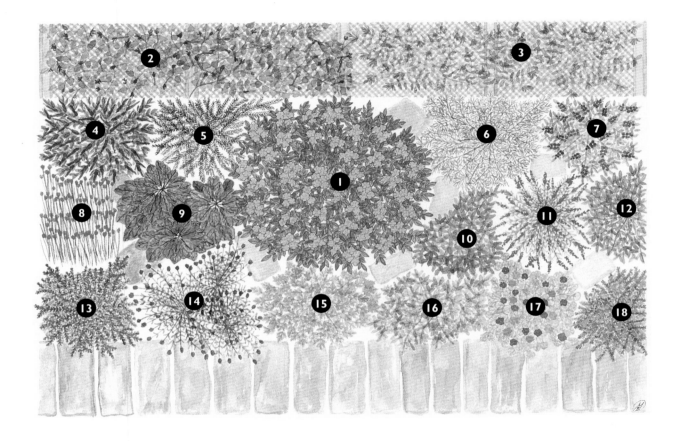

THE KITCHEN GARDEN

PLANT LIST

1. 'Frau Dagmar Hartopp' rose (*Rosa* 'Frau Dagmar Hartopp')

2. Scarlet runner bean (*Phaseolus coccineus*)

3. 'Cedar Lane' honeysuckle (*Lonicera sempervirens* 'Cedar Lane')

4. 'Thai Hot' pepper (*Capsicum annuum*)

5. Rosemary (*Rosmarinus officinalis*)

6. Bronze fennel (*Foeniculum vulgare* 'Smokey')

7. 'Sweet Chelsea' cherry tomato

8. Chives (*Allium schoenoprasum*)

9. 'Rhubarb Chard' Swiss chard

10. Sweet basil (*Ocimum basilicum*)

11. 'Provence' lavender (*Lavandula* × *intermedia* 'Provence')

12. Purple basil (*Ocimum basilicum* 'Red Rubin')

13. Compact Italian oregano (*Origanum vulgare* 'Compactum')

14. 'Strawberry Fields' globe amaranth (*Gomphrena* 'Strawberry Fields'); if desired, interplant 'Red Fire' leaf lettuce

15. Rose-scented geranium (*Pelargonium graveolens*)

16. 'Bergartten' sage (*Salvia officinalis* 'Bergartten')

17. 'Alaska Mixed' nasturtium (*Tropaeolum nanum* 'Alaska Mixed') and arugula

18. French thyme (*Thymus vulgaris*)

Even the smallest garden can accommodate a rose or two. The roses in this walled city garden are planted with foxglove penstemon and clematis.

CITY GARDEN:
A Narrow Bed of Roses and Companion Perennials

City gardens are quite often postage stamp–size yards with a narrow strip of bed along the side or front of the house. This tiny strip can be transformed into a garden beautifully planted with roses and perennials for season-long display. Even in a bed only 3 feet (1m) wide you can have a charming, though small, rose garden. Everblooming roses are a snap to keep in bounds with annual hard pruning in late winter.

Design Basics

A cascading carpet of 'The Fairy' rose anchors the corners at either end of the bed, forming a skirt studded with continuous, clear pink sweetheart blooms. Interplant the roses and edge the bed with low, soft, blue-flowered lesser calamint (*Calamintha nepeta*). Next, near each end of the bed, plant 'Betty Prior' roses for nonstop bloom. Clusters of carmine-pink, five-petaled flowers cover these rosebushes, which reach 4 feet (1.2m) in height. Between the sentinel 'Betty Prior' roses plant a sweep of lavender-flowered tall verbena (*Verbena bonariensis*) and face it with silver 'Powis Castle' artemisia. The foreground plants will flop a bit in a charming English cottage style.

This simple planting provides colorful pastel blooms from early summer until hard frost, and the flowers of verbena have the added benefit of attracting butterflies. If you're set on having early spring bloom in this garden strip, plant daffodils or other favorite bulbs under the tall verbena. As the bulb foliage dies back, the verbena will gradually fill the space and provide a succession of bloom.

🌹 Roses for the City Garden

Two of the most popular everblooming roses are included in this city garden design. 'Betty Prior' is a care-free floribunda with a robust habit. This lovely rose reaches about 4 feet (1.2m) in height and carries its single carmine flowers like bright butterflies all season long. One of the best-known small roses, 'The Fairy' performs well as a tough carpet, mounding to a height of about 2 feet (61cm) with a similar spread. It boasts handsome, shiny foliage and is studded with clusters of pink sweetheart blooms from mid-summer until frost.

THE CITY GARDEN
PLANT LIST

1. 'The Fairy' rose (*Rosa* 'The Fairy')

2. 'Betty Prior' rose (*R.* 'Betty Prior')

3. Lesser calamint (*Calamintha nepeta*)

4. Tall verbena (*Verbena bonariensis*)

5. 'Powis Castle' artemisia (*Artemisia* 'Powis Castle')

PATIO GARDEN:
Urns Full of Small Roses and Annuals

ABOVE: *Charming miniature roses fill a terra-cotta urn in this serene patio garden.*

❁

OPPOSITE: *Small roses and companion annuals displayed in urns and patio beds provide splashes of colorful flowers all summer long on a sunny patio, terrace, or deck.*

❁

Roses grown in tubs, pots, and urns create an attractive, colorful display all season long on patios, decks, or terraces. Miniature, sweetheart, patio, and other types of dwarf roses are excellent container subjects because they are extremely compact. However, with proper care—watering, potting up as needed, pruning, and fertilizing—almost any rose can be successfully grown in a container. The most important thing to remember is that the soil volume must be adequate for the rosebush's root system; if roots are crowded or constricted, the soil will dry out and the bush will die. For example, a miniature plug will easily fill a one-gallon (3.7l) container in the first growing season and then, depending on the plant's individual growth habit, it can be moved up to a larger container in succeeding growing seasons, ultimately finding a permanent home in the appropriate container. Root-bound bushes and plants that dry out quickly are indicators that soil volume is not adequate for the roots. Experiment with the roses that appeal to you and remember that small roses often prove to be the most practical for pot culture in terms of ease of maintenance, size, and weight of the pot.

Miniature roses propagated at home or purchased in 2-inch (5cm) pots can be grown in small containers and then transplanted to larger pots. But gardeners beware: when the 2-inch (5cm) pots arrive in the mail the roses all look tiny and cute, and it can be difficult to imagine the mature size of your rose plant. Therefore, it is important to find out the growth habit and mature size of individual varieties before you buy. Read the catalog description of the cultivar carefully or, if you are buying from a garden center, consult a reference book or experienced rose gardener to make sure that the rose you intend to purchase will not reach ungainly proportions.

For example, micro-miniature 'Cinderella' and dwarf China rose 'Roulettii' reach a mature size of only 12 inches (30cm). In contrast, climbing miniatures 'Red Cascade' and 'Jeanne Lajoie' develop into monsters that eventually outgrow all but the largest planters. Remember that container gardens are portable and the plants need not be permanent residents. As a young plant, the climbing miniature rose 'Red Cascade' can be attractively displayed in an urn, where it will shower its tiny scarlet blooms

over the rim. After a few seasons, when it becomes root bound, simply plant 'Red Cascade' in your garden and replant the urn with another miniature rose. Alternatively, you can prune the roots annually and continue to grow the climbing miniature in a large tub. Gardening is a forgiving art and as long as the plant receives adequate moisture and light, it is likely to survive.

One of the most beautiful ways to display small roses is to combine them with annuals, which bloom all summer. The following plans are full of simple combinations that provide colorful accents all summer in a sunny spot on your patio, deck, or terrace.

Lush pink roses and an
underplanting of 'Blue Dream'
linaria fill a cobalt
ceramic urn.

Design Basics

Gardening in containers is a great way to decorate your patio, deck, terrace, and garden walks. Use different types and sizes of containers, choosing those that appeal to you or that fit best with your garden style and design themes. Shop garden centers, flea markets, or specialty stores for half–barrels, terra-cotta pots, window boxes, stone urns, hollow tree stumps, brass pots, wrought-iron planters, or vintage kettles—almost anything can be used as a planter as long as it is equipped with drainage holes.

When designing your container garden, remember that placement and plant material can be formal or informal in style. For example, even the rustic half–barrel can contribute a formal element when planted with identical materials such as orange trees and set in rows or positioned in four corners on a patio. Although some homes are ideally suited for a formal urn display, most often you will want to create a wonderful mass effect, displaying pots filled with a variety of plants in attractive informal groupings.

And remember, the great advantage of a container garden is that it is a moveable composition. If you keep the pots light enough, you will be able to change the look of your patio or terrace in only a few minutes. You can then redesign your container garden at any time to highlight the peak bloom of a favorite plant, allow plants that have gone out of bloom for a while to recede into the background, and position bold foliage and beautiful containers where they can be best admired. Some pots are dramatic enough to stand alone and can be placed in strategic locations in sitting areas or in the garden to add a touch of romance, provide a focal point, or terminate a walk.

Choose a centerpiece for your pots: a standard rose or a plant with architectural foliage, such as canna, spiky dracena, banana, or a tall, graceful ornamental grass, makes an excellent focal point for almost any combination. Fill in around the centerpiece plant with annuals that spill over the brim and contribute foliage interest as well as colorful, cascading blooms. You may also enjoy planting some herbs and miniature or vining vegetables for a kitchen garden effect that is both beautiful and practical. Favorite roses can be grown as single specimens or combined with annuals to provide blooms all summer long.

The original everblooming patio rose, 'The Fairy' offers an abundant display of sweetheart roses for container gardens.
❀

🌹 Roses for the Patio Garden

The miniature rose 'Gourmet Popcorn' produces a continuous display of small double flowers that resemble popped corn. These spreading bushes grow 18 to 24 inches (46 to 61cm) high, and can be successfuly planted in a large urn. The containers look especially elegant edged with the delicate foliage and bright purple heads of 'Imagination' verbena, which will trail gracefully over the rim.

The fragrant miniature rose 'Sweet Chariot' offers its small purple blooms on spreading shrubs. For a lovely contrast, edge 'Sweet Chariot' with silver-leafed dwarf curry, and plant 'Needham Market' mini regal geraniums to throw scented leaves and pink flowers over the rim of the pot.

A dramatic effect can be had by combining the small russet flowers of 'Teddy Bear' miniature roses with the trailing foliage of 'Blackie' vining sweet potato (*Ipomoea batatas* 'Blackie') and 'Limelight' helichrysum (*Helichrysum petolare* 'Limelight'). Another simple mix pairs a bright yellow 'Rise 'n' Shine' miniature rose with 'Moe's Gold' helichrysum, a graceful edging plant.

One of the parents of modern miniatures, 'Roulettii' is an antique miniature China rose that adds a bright spot of color to the patio because it is always in bloom.

❁

Standard roses, or tree roses, are excellent candidates for container culture. Standards are roses that have been grafted high and appear to grow on a trunk. Particularly attractive are the weeping standards, roses with a naturally pendulous habit. 'The Fairy', a sweetheart rose with a graceful weeping habit, blooms continuously and can be planted as a standard in a large urn. For added interest, underplant 'The Fairy' with 'Pink Whirls' Cape marigolds and edge the pot with cascading drifts of 'Purple Wave' petunias. Both these flowering underplantings contrast handsomely with the warm pink roses of 'The Fairy'.

If you prefer a larger scale for your container garden, miniature roses can be used as edgings for bigger plants. In a large urn, plant South Pacific snowbush (*Breynia disticha* 'Roseo-picta') as the central element of your composition. Because it boasts kaleidoscopic foliage in shades of mottled white, green, burgundy, and pink, this unique tropical bush looks superb surrounded with a few spreading bushes of 'Green Ice' miniature rose. This rose's rare flower color always attracts attention: blooms open pearly white and change to soft, cool green. In keeping with the theme of a white container garden, interplant 'Green Ice' roses with the eye-catching, pendulous trusses of 'Whirligig' Cape marigolds, which bear pure white flowers that resemble pinwheels marked with purple eyes. Finish your container by planting helichrysum around the edge, allowing the plant's rounded, silver, woolly leaves to drape elegantly over the rim.

Another useful edging dwarf is the China rose 'Roulettii'. Combine it with the large, textured, silver leaves of the mint relative plectranthus (*Plectranthus argentea*), and plant a trailing small-flowered petunia (*Petunia integrifolia*) to throw its bright magenta blooms over the rim all season long.

THE PATIO GARDEN

PLANT LIST I

1. 'Gourmet Popcorn' rose (*Rosa* 'Gourmet Popcorn')

2. 'Imagination' verbena (*Verbena* 'Imagination')

PLANT LIST II

3. 'Teddy Bear' rose (*R.* 'Teddy Bear')

4. 'Blackie' vining sweet potato (*Ipomoea batatas* 'Blackie')

5. 'Limelight' helichrysum (*Helichrysum petolare* 'Limelight')

PLANT LIST III

6. Snowbush (*Breynia disticha* 'Roseo-picta')

7. 'Green Ice' rose (*R.* 'Green Ice')

8. Helichrysum (*Helichrysum petolare*)

9. 'Whirligig' Cape marigold (*Osteosperum ecklonis* 'Whirligig')

PLANT LIST IV

10. 'Rise 'n' Shine' rose (*R.* 'Rise 'n' Shine')

11. 'Moe's Gold' helichrysum (*Helichrysum argyrophyllum* 'Moe's Gold')

PLANT LIST V

12. 'The Fairy' weeping standard (*R.* 'The Fairy')

13. 'Pink Whirls' Cape marigold (*Osteosperum ecklonis* 'Pink Whirls')

14. 'Purple Wave' petunia (*Petunia* 'Purple Wave')

PLANT LIST VI

15. 'Sweet Chariot' rose (*R.* 'Sweet Chariot')

16. Dwarf curry plant (*Helichrysum angustifolium nana*)

17. 'Needham Market' mini regal geranium (*Pelargonium* 'Needham Market')

PLANT LIST VII

18. Menthol plant (*Plectranthus argentea*)

19. 'Roulettii' rose (*R.* 'Roulettii')

20. Petunia (*Petunia integrifolia*)

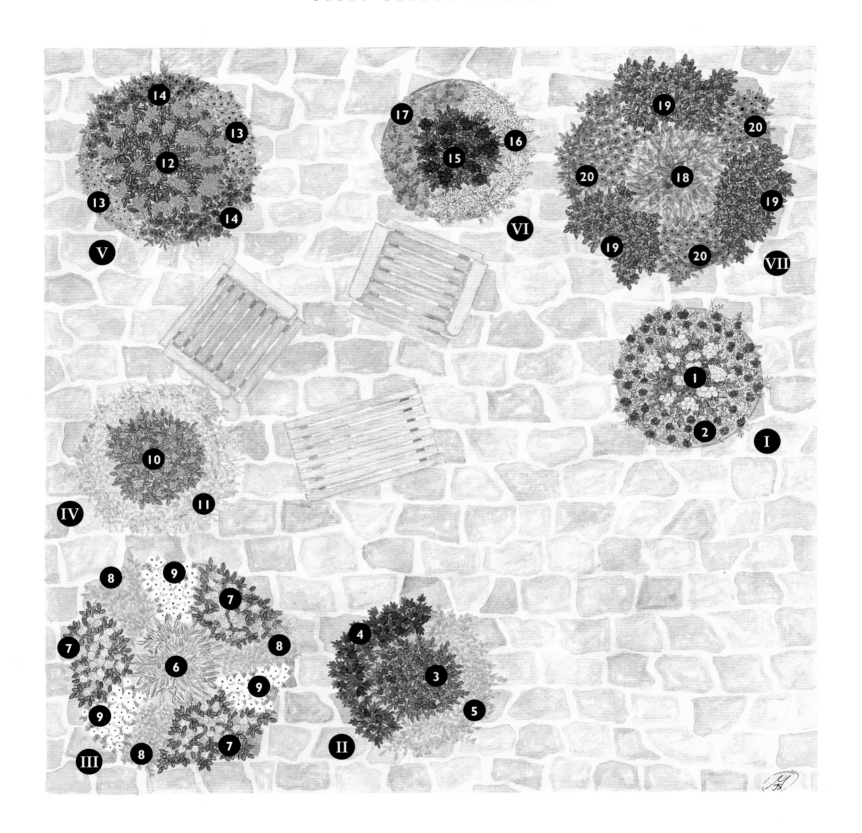

COTTAGE GARDEN:
Two Designs for Roses and Companion Perennials in an Informal English Style

In the cottage garden the relaxed artfulness of nature guides the gardener's hand. The serene arrangement of plants is so simple that it looks effortless, even neglected. English garden writer Reginald Farrer reminds us that this offhand style is the true ambition of the gardener—as in all great art, the artistry is concealed. He also wisely advises that "right letting alone and right meddling are the beginning and ending of good gardening." In the cottage garden this usually means observing and then enhancing the special characteristics, life cycles, and self-sowing habits of your plants.

Learning to identify seedlings of self-sowing annuals, for example, allows you to appreciate their chance movements, which sometimes create happy accidents: wonderful plant combinations that provide subtle changes from year to year. However, the hand of the gardener is ever at work, so feel free to sow seeds, pull and move seedlings, and thin them so that they appear like the natural drifts of wildflowers in a meadow. And don't hesitate to rip out any plants that aren't doing their jobs.

❀ Design Basics

The plan for this cottage garden shows a small yard bisected by a stepping-stone path that is long enough to wind a bit, drawing the eye along its rustic curve. The path is flanked by unpretentious, almost wild, plantings in irregular beds. Typically, low-growing edging plants—rose campion, cranesbill, and lady's mantle—are situated in the front of the bed, gracefully spilling out over the path, while medium and taller perennials and shrubs are layered toward the back. But don't rule out placing "see-through" plants such as Japanese anemone, catmint, lavender mist, poppies, butterfly weed, daylilies, and lilies in mid- to foreground positions, thereby varying height and providing a more natural, meadowlike appearance.

One small specimen tree in the cottage garden can provide a focal point of all-season interest. The beautiful Korean stewartia (*Stewartia koreana*), with its camellialike summer flowers, excellent orange-red autumn foliage, and attractive reddish flaking bark, is an excellent choice. Kousa dogwood

OPPOSITE: This classic cottage garden overflows with a profusion of roses, poppies, geraniums, and catmint. Achieving this unstudied look involves some thoughtful planning.
❀

(*Cornus kousa*) offers similar ornamental characteristics, as does the elegant paperbark maple (*Acer griseum*). Handsome native juneberry, or shadbush (*Amelanchier arborea*), produces white, starlike flowers in early spring (when the shad run), even before it leafs out; its fruits, which appear in summer, are attractive to birds, while its orange-red autumn color is an added bonus. Select one of these four-star specimen trees to plant in your cottage garden, or choose your own favorite flowering tree.

In addition to masses of glorious roses, both these cottage garden plans provide fragrant, early-season shrubs, lots of summer and autumn flowers, fall foliage color, and winter interest.

Cottage Garden in Cool Pastels: Heritage Roses and Old-Fashioned Perennials

The blowsy, fragrant heritage roses, which have long been traditional companions for old-fashioned perennial flowers, are a perfect choice for cottage gardens. Situated among herbaceous neighbors, the scented flowers, recurrent bloom, and colorful rose hips of antique roses are enhanced, while imperfections—especially leaf problems—are attractively concealed by sumptuous drifts of perennials. Country flowers such as foxgloves, cottage pinks, perennial geraniums, alliums, lilies, butterfly bushes, and ornamental herbs blend easily with the muted pastels of the white, blush, pink, and magenta-red antique roses.

All blue-flowered herbs, but especially lavender, salvia, and catmint, look exquisite with roses in this scheme, and add their fragrant leaves to the garden's essence. Silver foliage plants—including artemisia, thyme,

ABOVE: *Though 'Ballerina' is a modern shrub rose, it has an old-fashioned look and mixes well with antique roses and old-fashioned perennials.*

❀

BELOW, LEFT: *'Konigin von Danemark' is an aristocratic heritage rose for the cottage garden, and blends beautifully with foxglove, allium, and violet sage.*

❀

OPPOSITE: *Multiflora rose grows up a rustic wooden pergola in this informal English garden; planted beside the pergola is an array of companion perennials, including delphiniums, foxgloves, and catmint.*

❀

and lavender—also enhance the display, playing off the pastel-colored antique roses, with their soft pink to deep violet-red blooms. Silver-leaved plants also provide a good transition—a resting place for the eye—between diverse groups of flowers.

Roses for the Pastel Cottage Garden

Some of the most fragrant and beautiful roses give their all for several weeks in June, overwhelming with their beauty; then they quietly become part of the green background. Alba roses are hardy survivors, and their lavish, fragrant June blooms make a great centerpiece for the cottage garden. 'Konigin von Danemark', one such alba rose, is a graceful bush that grows to about 4 feet (1.2m) tall and wide. Its showy, full flowers are quartered and have a charming buttonlike center; the soft pink flowers exude a heavy yet delightful perfume. This aristocratic shrub rose looks particularly beautiful in combination with violet, blue, or magenta flowers and gray-leaved perennials.

Wild, or species, roses belong to the antique rose group and add a special natural effect to the cottage garden. Offering interesting foliage, flowers, fruits, and autumn color, both red-leaved rose (*Rosa glauca*) and New England shining rose (*R. nitida*) are must-have plants. When surrounded by old-fashioned perennials, these two species roses look attractive throughout the year.

You'll notice that the distinctive foliage of red-leaved rose, with its remarkable burgundy-tinged, blue-gray leaves, creates an attractive contrast to the plant's red stems. Small, pink, star-shaped flowers with white eyes stud the canes in late spring; orange hips ripen in late summer; and the mahogany-red stems are effective through winter. Underplant red-leaved roses with artemisia for a wonderful contrast to rose flowers, foliage, and hips.

The smallest of the native East Coast roses, New England shining rose bears deep pink, fragrant flowers followed by red hips. The leaves are small and glossy, giving this rose its common name, and they color to a striking scarlet in autumn. 'Corylus' is a hybrid—between New England shining rose and rugosa rose—that is particularly heat tolerant, and is ideal for regions where summers are hot. Position 'Corylus' near the front of the border, where its fragrant single blooms of deep pink look attractive fringed with herbaceous companions such as star of Persia allium and salvia in the spring and Japanese anemones in the autumn.

OPPOSITE: *A planting in the cottage garden tradition might include a few cherished roses by the kitchen door, a bank of fragrant roses along a path, or the natural, almost neglected look of a wildflower meadow.*

BELOW: *'Alchymist' is a great once-blooming climber with charming, old-fashioned flowers.*

Bred from a modern climber and the wild sweetbrier rose, 'Alchymist', with its lax habit and long canes, makes a glorious wall shrub or climber for a trellis, fence, or pillar. Although not technically an antique rose, 'Alchymist' is treasured for its large, old-fashioned, soft apricot flowers that exude a wonderful perfume and for its magnificent early-summer flower display. In the plan shown, it is trained up the right side of a rose arch that adorns the back garden gate, but 'Alchymist' also makes an elegant specimen rose. Don't let its short bloom time prevent you from growing this exquisite beauty; simply intertwine a small-flowered clematis, such as the purple Italian clematis 'Etoile Violette', over the rose canes to extend the bloom through summer. You can also train goldflame honeysuckle up the left side of the rose arch to meet 'Alchymist' halfway. Goldflame honeysuckle will effectively carry the bloom on your rose arch through the summer with a tangle of delightful, fragrant, tubular, carmine-gold flowers that change to pink.

Heritage roses that offer repeat bloom in late summer and autumn are especially prized because they add a rare touch of elegance to the cottage garden, but without the huge, showy flowers or stiff, upright habit of the hybrid teas. Among the most compact and hardy of heritage roses is 'Rose de Rescht', a fragrant damask perpetual. Its brilliant fuchsia-violet, scented blooms feature many packed petals, which cover the small bush in late spring and again in late summer and autumn. 'Rose de Rescht' always looks at home nestled among old-fashioned herbaceous companions and faced with a skirt of cottage pinks or geraniums.

To complete this pastel cottage garden design, plant hybrid musk rose 'Ballerina', which bears dainty, single, bicolor flowers in large clusters that resemble its multiflora rose parent. 'Ballerina' is a modern shrub rose that is easy to integrate with antique roses and old-fashioned perennials, and is valued for its disease resistance and repeat bloom. You might choose to use it as a low-growing, mounding shrub underplanted with fragrant lavender. It's easy to keep 'Ballerina' in bounds if you prune it hard every year.

After the big rose display in the cottage garden is over, summer-blooming lilies, butterfly bush, annuals, and the autumn flowers of Japanese anemones pick up the bloom and carry it through till hard frost. The hips and mahogany-red stems of red-leaved rose will attract birds to the garden and

provide winter interest. You can create additional winter beauty by incorporating winterberry holly, and evergreen Christmas and Lenten roses, which often start blooming while there is still snow cover. Fragrant viburnum adds its spring bloom of sweetly scented, pink-tinged flowers. Its handsome glossy foliage is also an asset through the summer, coloring to golden yellow in the autumn. For a colorful display in early spring before your roses are blooming, plant favorite bulbs under the shrubs and among summer-blooming perennials. By using such a variety of plants you'll create a succession of flowers that will keep your cottage garden looking beautiful from the first bloom of the hellebores through the glory of the roses to the colorful autumn foliage and winter berries.

THE PASTEL COTTAGE GARDEN

PLANT LIST

1. 'Konigin von Danemark' rose (*Rosa* 'Konigin von Danemark')

2. Red-leaved rose (*R. glauca*)

3. 'Corylus' New England shining rose (*R. nitida* 'Corylus')

4. Rose arch right side: 'Alchymist' rose (*R.* 'Alchymist') and 'Etoile Violette' Italian clematis (*Clematis viticella* 'Etoile Violette'); left side: goldflame honeysuckle (*Lonicera heckrottii*)

5. 'Rose de Rescht' rose (*R.* 'Rose de Rescht')

6. 'Ballerina' rose (*R.* 'Ballerina')

7. Korean stewartia (*Stewartia koreana*)

8. Compact fragrant viburnum (*Viburnum carlesii* 'Compactum')

9. 'Nanho Blue' butterfly bush (*Buddleia davidii* 'Nanho Blue')

10. Christmas rose and Lenten rose (*Helleborus niger* and *H. orientalis*)

11. Foxglove (*Digitalis purpurea*) and regal lilies (*Lilium regale*)

12. Siberian catmint (*Nepeta sibirica* 'Souvenir d'André Chaudron')

13. Star-of-Persia allium (*Allium christophii*) and 'Queen Charlotte' Japanese anemone (*Anemone* × *hybrida* 'Queen Charlotte')

14. Rose campion (*Lychnis coronaria*)

15. Himalayan perennial geranium (*Geranium himalayense*)

16. 'Provence' lavender (*Lavandula* × *intermedia* 'Provence')

17. Lavender mist (*Thalictrum rochebrunianum* 'Lavender Mist')

18. Lady's mantle (*Alchemilla glaucescens*)

19. 'Montrose Ruby' heuchera (*Heuchera* × 'Montrose Ruby')

20. 'Huntington Gardens' artemisia (*Artemisia* 'Huntington Gardens')

21. Violet sage (*Salvia nemorosa* 'Viola Klose')

22. Love-in-a-mist (*Nigella damascena*) and 'Homestead Purple' verbena (*Verbena canadensis* 'Homestead Purple')

23. Shirley poppies (*Papaver rhoeas* 'Mother of Pearl'); if desired, interplant 'Sonata Dwarf Mixed' cosmos (*Cosmos bipinnatus* 'Sonata Dwarf Mixed')

24. Tall verbena (*Verbena bonariensis*)

Cottage Garden in Hot Sunset Colors:
Shrub Roses and Perennials in Yellow, Orange, and Scarlet

If your yard has blooms only in spring and then suffers from summer doldrums, perk it up with a strong, brilliant color scheme. Choose a hot palette, dominated by sunset colors in yellow, orange, and scarlet, for your cottage garden. With this plan you'll enjoy peak bloom from late spring until hard frost and interesting autumn foliage and winter beauty.

❧ Roses for the Sunset-Colored Cottage Garden

An old favorite, 'Harison's Yellow' rose, produces a profusion of semidouble, cupped, deep yellow flowers with golden yellow stamens in late spring and early summer. This hardy shrub has an upright habit and grows to about 5 feet (1.5m), and its fernlike, blue-green foliage is attractive even when the flowers are not in bloom. 'Harison's Yellow' looks stunning grown with 'Bonfire' orange-red oriental poppies and underplanted with cool violet-blue 'New Hampshire Purple' cranesbill.

'Harison's Yellow' is highly desired for its deep yellow blooms.
❀

Tangerine-flowered 'Westerland' rose also finds a home in the sunset-colored cottage garden. In this plan, it is trained up one side of a rose arch that stands at the back garden gate. You can also grow 'Westerland' on a freestanding pillar or obelisk to provide height and a colorful focal point. Train the small-flowered red clematis 'Madame Julia Correvon' to grow over it. The clematis offers its blooms well into the autumn and contributes a distinctive contrast to the tangerine-colored rose flowers. Both the rose and clematis repeat their bloom in late summer and autumn. You can also train trumpet honeysuckle (*Lonicera sempervirens* 'Cedar Lane') up the other side of the arch to meet 'Westerland' and enhance bloom through summer with fragrant, deep red, tubular flowers.

English roses 'Lilian Austin' in salmon or 'Graham Thomas' in clear yellow add their large, bright, fragrant flowers to the early-summer display and provide some welcome repeat bloom in late summer and autumn as well. 'Graham Thomas' achieves some height and has a rather stiffly upright habit similar to that of a hybrid tea. For this reason, you'll want to place it in the mid- to background and surround it with perennials. 'Lilian Austin' is a more relaxed shrub, and can take her place in the midground underplanted with yellow horned poppy.

To complete the rose planting, put in everblooming floribunda roses: 'Playboy' sports clusters of large, showy, orange blooms with only five petals; or try 'Sunsprite', a floribunda laden with sprays of clear yellow flowers that exude a sweet fragrance. 'Showbiz' offers eye-catching scarlet blooms on dense, low-spreading bushes. These roses are shown to advantage blended with herbaceous seasonal companions: poppies, peonies, coreopsis, daylilies, lilies, daisies, and goldenrod, for bright floral displays from spring until hard frost. Plant your favorite spring bulbs to start things off in late winter and early spring and include a few annuals for a quick flash of color.

A planting of shrubs with interesting foliage will greatly enhance the sunset cottage garden. The lemon-colored foliage of 'Worcester Gold' caryopteris adds attractive leaves and blue flowers, making a bold contrast to the dark bronze foliage of neighboring companions such as 'Mohrchen' sedum and purple spurge. Meanwhile 'Albury Purple' hypericum contributes bright yellow flowers handsomely displayed against burgundy foliage, followed by orange fruits. 'J.L. Pennock' enkianthus is a compact rhododendron relative that thrives in sun. Its lovely bell-shaped flowers appear in the spring before its small leaves, which color to a spectacular scarlet in autumn. A tiered branching pattern gives this connoisseurs plant an Oriental demeanor.

For an evergreen foliage effect, plant gold-tipped Cripps Hinoki false cypress and train golden clematis to grow over it. This easy-to-grow, unusual clematis will throw its thimble-size yellow blooms over the tree in summer and add globes of hairlike, silky fruits in autumn.

ABOVE, FROM LEFT TO RIGHT:
'Graham Thomas', 'Lilian Austin', 'Playboy'.
❀

THE SUNSET COTTAGE GARDEN

PLANT LIST

1. 'Lilian Austin' rose (*Rosa* 'Lilian Austin') or 'Graham Thomas' rose (*R.* 'Graham Thomas')

2. 'Harison's Yellow' rose (*R.* 'Harison's Yellow')

3. 'Playboy' rose (*R.* 'Playboy') or 'Sunsprite' rose (*R.* 'Sunsprite')

4. Rose arch right side: 'Westerland' rose (*R.* 'Westerland') and 'Madame Julia Correvon' clematis (*Clematis* 'Madame Julia Correvon'); left side: trumpet honeysuckle (*Lonicera sempervirens* 'Cedar Lane')

5. 'Showbiz' rose (*R.* 'Showbiz')

6. Paperbark maple (*Acer griseum*)

7. 'J. L. Pennock' enkianthus (*Enkianthus perulatus* 'J. L. Pennock')

8. Cripps Hinoki false cypress (*Chamaecyparis obtusa* 'Crippsii') and golden clematis (*Clematis tangutica*)

9. 'Albury Purple' hypericum (*Hypericum inodorum* 'Albury Purple')

10. 'Scarlet O'Hara' peony (*Paeonia lactiflora* 'Scarlet O'Hara')

11. 'Worcester Gold' caryopteris (*Caryopteris* × *clandonensis* 'Worcester Gold')

12. Christmas rose and Lenten rose (*Helleborus niger* and *H. orientalis*)

13. 'Bonfire' oriental poppy (*Papaver orientalis* 'Bonfire') and butterfly weed (*Asclepias curassavica*)

14. 'New Hampshire Purple' perennial geranium (*Geranium pratense* 'New Hampshire Purple')

15. 'Hyperion' daylily (*Hemerocallis* 'Hyperion')

16. Horned poppy (*Glaucium flavum*)

17. 'Mohrchen' stonecrop (*Sedum* 'Mohrchen')

18. Purple spurge (*Euphorbia amygaloides* 'Purpurea')

19. Carolina lupine (*Thermopsis caroliniana*)

20. Lily leek (*Allium moly*) and 'Lady in Red' sage (*Salvia coccinea* 'Lady in Red')

21. 'Summer Sun' false sunflower (*Heliopsis helianthoides* 'Summer Sun')

22. Henry lily (*Lilium henryi*) and 'Fireworks' goldenrod (*Solidago rugosa* 'Fireworks')

23. California poppy (*Eschscholzia californica*) and 'Scarlet Poncho' coleus (*Coleus* 'Scarlet Poncho')

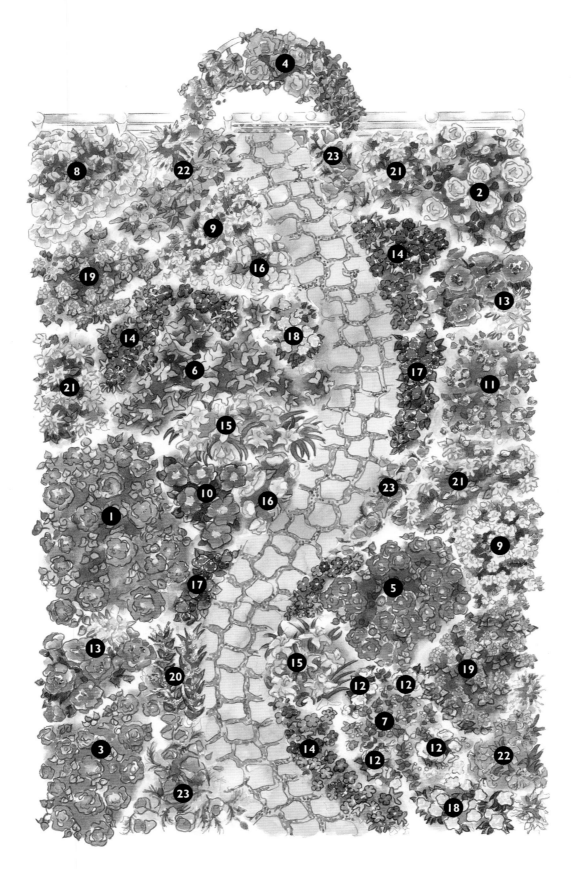

ROCK WALL GARDEN:
A Dry Stone Wall Carpeted with Flowers

Roses cascading over stone make a lovely seasonal garden picture. The easy-care prostrate rose 'White Meidiland' is a great selection for the rock wall garden.

Plants nestled in rock crevices provide a pleasing organic beauty. If you wish to imitate nature's rock gardens, creating a good home for alpine and mountain plants, a rock wall garden is the perfect choice for you. A dry stone wall—one built using a soil fill without mortar—furnishes the perfect environment for alpines, and the view of foliage and flowers draped over stone is refreshingly different from that of a level border. Dry stone walls are naturally well drained, and the cool planting pockets between the rocks simulate growing conditions in mountain habitats. Alpines and mountain plant species that are often difficult to grow in borders because of wet winter soil conditions will thrive in the rock wall garden.

Design Basics

The taller the wall, the more dramatic the garden; but a low rock wall also offers wonderful possibilities for planting schemes. Even a mortared or brick retaining wall promises unusual opportunities for vertical gardening: floppy groundcover roses, clematis, winter jasmine, and carpet junipers can be planted at the top of the wall to gracefully drape rocks or bricks with colorful flowers and foliage. Chinks in the mortar provide tiny planting pockets for stonecrops, hens-and-chicks, and mat-forming alpines, herbs, and self-sowing perennials that require little soil to thrive. Where soil pockets exist, ephemeral bulbs and annuals can be planted to provide seasonal color. Finally, you can add long-blooming perennials to the bed at the top of the wall for a deep, layered look.

Large sweeps of select rock plant species displayed in naturalistic drifts bring a subtle kind of beauty to the dry rock wall garden. Patterns, colors, and textures of a few dominant plant groups repeated in each season coordinate the garden design throughout the year. Even viewed from a distance, many small-flowered common mountain species such as basket-of-gold and rock cress provide a showy floral display in the spring and make a strong textural statement with their silver or dark evergreen foliage in other seasons. Roses and mat-forming herbs such as thyme offer early summer color. From summer on, drifts of silver-leaved santolina, rock rose, and artemisia species provide soft gray-textured foliage that acts as a visual anchor and holds the design together through the autumn. Two reliable summer companions in the rock wall are 'Moonbeam' coreopsis and 'Butterfly Blue' scabiosa; a prostrate daisy-flowered chrysanthemum supplies autumn blooms. Trailing annuals supplement the summer and autumn perennial display.

Roses edged with flowering herbs grace the top of a rock wall.

Roses for the Rock Wall Garden

Roses with mounding and prostrate habits, such as 'Stanwell Perpetual', 'Red Cascade', and 'Snow Carpet', are superior selections for the rock wall garden. Plant them at the top of the wall and allow them to throw their eye-catching blooms over the rock face. Enjoy the sweet scent of the soft blush 'Stanwell Perpetual' blooms at nose level. Micro-miniature roses such as 'Cinderella', 'Si', 'Live Wire', and 'Red Minimo', and spreading miniatures 'Green Ice' and 'Sweet Chariot' also find a home in the sunny wall garden.

THE ROCK WALL GARDEN

PLANT LIST

1. 'Stanwell Perpetual' rose (*Rosa* 'Stanwell Perpetual')

2. 'Snow Carpet' rose (*R.* 'Snow Carpet')

3. 'Cinderella' rose (*R.* 'Cinderella')

4. 'Ivory Jewel' peony (*Paeonia lactiflora* 'Ivory Jewel')

5. 'Persimmon' Siberian iris (*Iris sibirica* 'Persimmon')

6. 'Blue Hill' sage (*Salvia nemorosa* 'Blue Hill')

7. 'Moonshine' yarrow (*Achillea* × 'Moonshine')

8. 'Sulphurea' basket-of-gold (*Aurinia saxatilis* 'Sulphurea')

9. Purple rock cress (*Aubrieta* × *hybrida* 'Whitewell Gem')

10. 'Autumn Snow' candytuft (*Iberis sempervirens* 'Autumn Snow')

11. Mountain pinks (*Phlox subulata* 'Emerald Cushion Blue')

12. Pincushion spurge (*Euphorbia polychroma*)

13. Yellow bleeding heart (*Corydalis lutea*)

14. Dwarf lavender cotton (*Santolina incana nana*)

15. Thyme (*Thymus praecox* 'Minor')

16. 'Dragon's Blood' stonecrop (*Sedum spurium* 'Dragon's Blood')

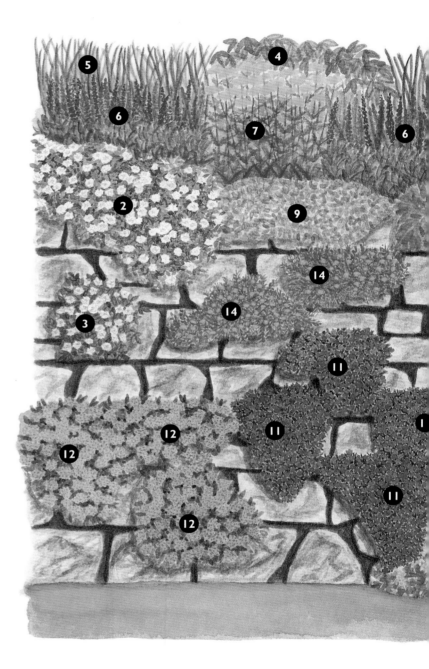

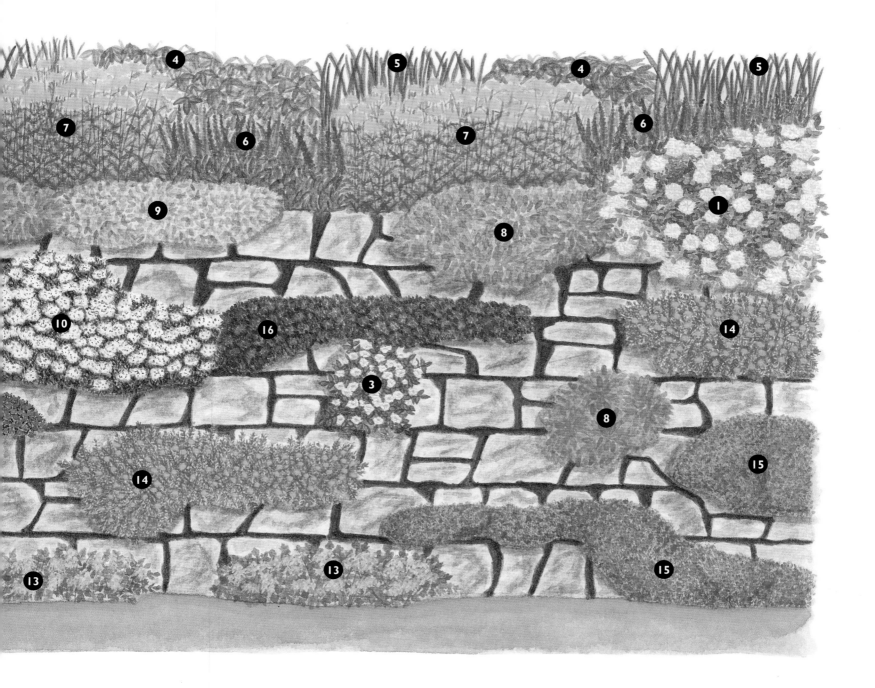

EIGHTEENTH-CENTURY COUNTRY GARDEN: Period Garden circa 1780

Thomas Jefferson laid out the gardens at Monticello, his home in Virginia, between 1772 and 1809. Unlike the gardens at colonial Williamsburg, which were influenced by the formal French parterre style, the Monticello gardens reflect the naturalistic style associated with the English landscape garden tradition. Jefferson's plantation was sited on a mountaintop that offered commanding views in all directions. Initially, he opened vistas, planted copses of trees and screened shrubberies, created a deer park, and planted a series of terraced vegetable gardens. He naturalized shrubs, bulbs, and wildflowers, and made great expanses of lawn.

A plant enthusiast who grew a wide range of trees, shrubs, and flowers, Jefferson planned a series of oval flower gardens bordering a roundabout walk at the back of the house. The flower gardens at Monticello provide excellent examples of plants used in eighteenth-century North American gardens. Plants selected by Jefferson had to meet his stern criteria: they had to be either exceptionally handsome or fragrant. His detailed garden records provide invaluable data on the plants grown at Monticello and also made possible the restoration of the flower gardens in 1940.

Design Basics

This plan for an eighteenth-country garden combines naturalized plantings with colorful masses of annuals, drifts of perennials, and bulbs laid out in a simple oval bed. The bed is located at the edge of the woodland and the back part of the bed is in the high shade of large deciduous trees such as honey

ABOVE: 'Rosa Mundi' is a very old gallica rose often grown in eighteenth-century American gardens.

OPPOSITE: You may wish to interpret a period garden more loosely, and include some of your favorite new cultivars as well as antique plants. Feel free to mix and match, but keep in mind that newer varieties with an old-fashioned look will combine with old garden plants more naturally than exotic-looking introductions.

locust or willow oak. The woodland understory is filled with redbud, dogwood, and rose bay rhododendron. Wild roses are positioned at the woodland edge at the back of the bed; lilies, bluebells, and columbines are naturalized around them. The more compact roses, perennials, and annuals are grouped toward the middle and foreground of the bed in full sun. Cool season annuals such as poppies and sweet William are succeeded by summer-blooming ones and spring bulbs are interplanted with lilies, extending the display of flowers from early spring until hard frost. All of the flowers used in the eighteenth-century country garden plan were in cultivation in the United States by 1780 and were grown at Monticello.

Roses for the Eighteenth-Century Country Garden

Roses grown in the eighteenth-century country garden include many of the charming old European types brought to North America by the settlers. At Monticello, Jefferson cultivated some cherished antique roses that are still favored in modern gardens today. Some of these are the stunning striped gallica 'Rosa Mundi'; the pure white, fragrant rose 'Alba Semi-Plena'; the fragrant many-petaled 'Common Moss'; and 'Autumn Damask', which was treasured by eighteenth-century gardeners for its repeat bloom.

European wild roses also find a home in the eighteenth-century garden: sweetbriar, or eglantine rose (*Rosa eglanteria*), boasts fragrant, apple-scented foliage and single, pink flowers followed by small red hips. Jefferson naturalized sweetbriar on his estate, and indeed, many other eighteenth-century gardeners must have planted this favorite European rose, because it has escaped cultivation and is found growing wild throughout North America. He also grew the free-flowering Scotch briar (*R. spinosissima*), which bears creamy, single flowers and distinctive blue-black hips. By the turn of the century, Jefferson was also growing several roses native to North America. All of these roses are extremely hardy and disease-free.

Flowers for the Eighteenth-Century Country Garden

Both exotic and native flora were grown at Monticello, and Jefferson received plants and seeds from abroad and from the areas around his home. He appreciated lilies and grew the fragrant Madonna lily, one of the world's oldest cultivated plants, which was brought to North America by the Puritans. He

Sweetbriar rose (Rosa eglanteria) was first brought to America by European settlers and was planted by Thomas Jefferson at Monticello.

Native plants, such as these black-eyed Susans, are perfectly suited to an eighteenth-century country garden. Explore the plants native to your area, and experiment with them in your old-fashioned garden.

also planted the elegant native Canada lily, with its clear yellow summer flowers, and the Allegheny Turk's cap lily, which he admired in a friend's garden in Richmond. Other native wildflowers valued as garden plants by Jefferson and other eighteenth-century gardeners include columbine, cardinal flower, and Virginia bluebell. Spring bulbs such as pasqueflower, daffodil, and hyacinth, brought over by the Europeans who settled on the East Coast, were treasured in colonial America. At Monticello, annuals planted for summer color abound, including corn poppies, four-o'clocks, stocks, globe amaranth, sweet Williams, hollyhocks, snapdragons, and heliotrope. Many of these beautiful and fragrant old-fashioned flowers are still among the most popular annuals grown today.

EIGHTEENTH-CENTURY COUNTRY GARDEN

PLANT LIST

1. Sweetbriar, or elgantine rose (*R. eglanteria*)

2. Scotch briar (*R. spinosissima*)

3. 'Alba Semi-Plena' rose (*R.* 'Alba Semi-Plena')

4. 'Common Moss' rose, also known as 'Communis' or 'Centifolia Muscosa' (*R. centifolia* 'Common Moss')

5. 'Autumn Damask' rose (*R.* 'Autumn Damask', also known as *R. damascena* var. *semperflorens*)

6. 'Rosa Mundi' rose (*R.* 'Rosa Mundi', also known as *R. gallica* var. *versicolor*)

7. Peony (*Paeonia officinalis*)

8. Black hollyhock (*Alcea rosea* 'Niger')

9. Madonna lily (*Lilium candidum*)

10. Virginia bluebells (*Mertensia virginica*) and Canadian lily (*Lilium canadense*)

11. Wild columbine (*Aquilegia canadensis*) and Turk's cap lily (*Lilium superbum*)

12. Blackberry lily (*Belamcanda chinensis*) and daffodil (*Narcissus* spp.)

13. Bearded iris (*Iris* × *germanica*)

14. Corn poppy (*Papaver rhoeas*) and heliotrope (*Heliotropium arborescens*)

15. Sweet William (*Dianthus barbatus*) and globe amaranth (*Gomphrena globosa*)

16. Four-o'clock (*Mirabilis jalapa*) and hyacinth (*Hyacinthus orientalis*)

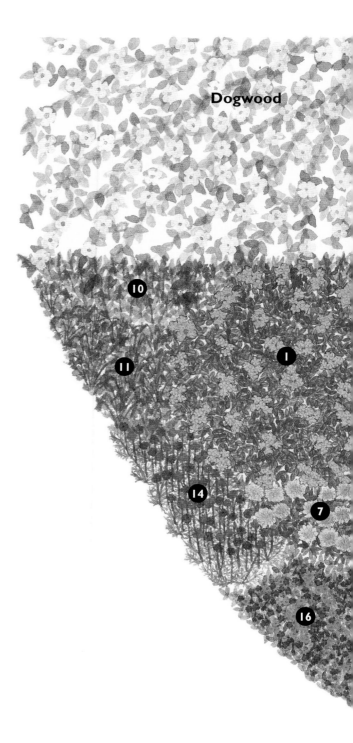

Dogwood

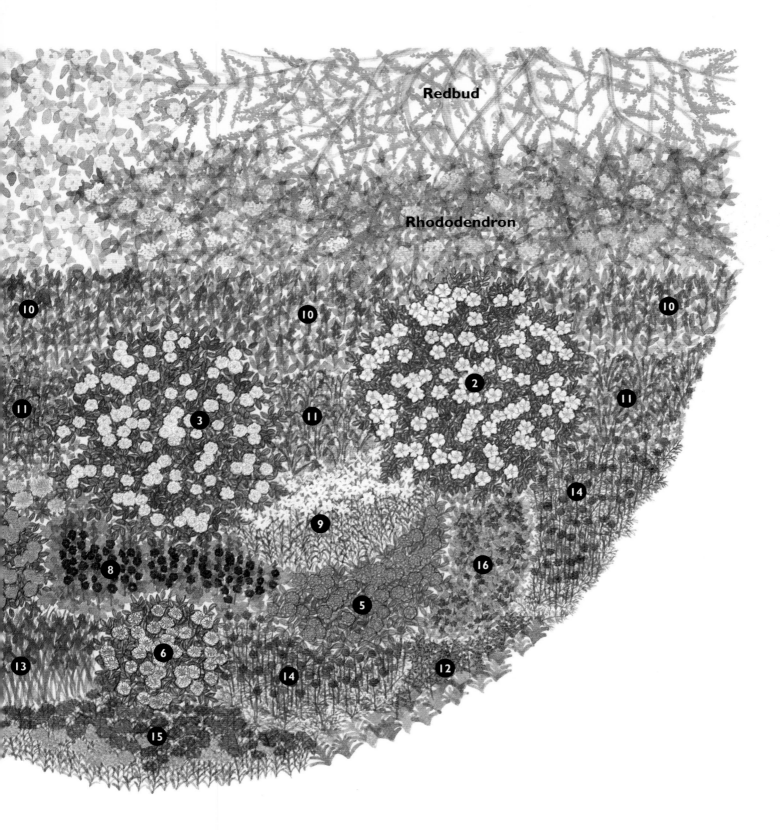

Redbud

Rhododendron

MIXED BORDER GARDENS IN SINGLE COLORS

English garden designer Gertrude Jekyll looked at the garden with an artist's eye and used plantings as a canvas for her color work with flowers and foliage. In her book *Color Schemes for the Flower Garden*, published in 1908, she put forth unique ideas about the use of color and suggested wonderful color combinations based on her vast knowledge of plants and her experience as a painter. She perfected the sunset-colored border and also introduced the concept of gardens in which a single color scheme dominates. Although Jekyll did not have room to plant all of the monochromatic schemes she had in mind, she designed a series of blue, gray, green, orange, and gold gardens. Yet she was not a slave to her theme, simply throwing together blue flowers because they were blue. On the contrary, Jekyll's highest priority was creating beauty through the blending of form, foliage, and flowers; she also observed that her blue flowers were enhanced by a complementary color such as pale yellow or white.

Jekyll mapped out the gardens of special coloring in her book and hoped that other gardeners of like mind would plant them, and so they did. We are indebted to those who followed her lead and created wonderful garden rooms and mixed borders in special colors that still thrive today, most notably in the National Trust gardens at Hidcote Manor and Sissinghurst Castle in England.

The Red Border

Inspired by the famous red borders at Hidcote Manor, this garden design is full of luscious scarlet and orange-red flowers. The bright hues are shown to advantage set against a green backdrop highlighted with burgundy foliage plants.

Design Basics

Purple smokebush and purple-leaved elderberry contribute their burgundy foliage, which makes an excellent foil for bright roses and perennial flowers. Grow these bushes as cut-back shrubs by copicing, a method of pruning in which trees and shrubs are cut back hard in late winter or early spring so that their size is strictly managed and they do not outgrow the border.

OPPOSITE: Choosing a single-color theme for your garden grants it an automatic cohesiveness. This white border is striking at any time of day, and is particularly beautiful when viewed by moonlight.

❀

'Betty Prior' is an excellent
choice for small-space gardens because its carmine
flowers bloom
almost nonstop.
❀

Many burgundy-leaved herbaceous plants add their bronze foliage to the mix, including 'Jungle Beauty' ajuga, 'Chocolate Ruffles' heuchera, purple-leaved spurge, and red-leaved ornamental grass. Annuals such as 'Red Shield' hibiscus, red-leaf alternanthera, bronze-leaved dahlias, red-foliage cannas, and coleus are also striking in the red border. For early flowering, underplant summer-blooming perennials such as daylilies, crocosmia, and lilies with early red species-type tulips, or use your favorite spring bulbs.

The large, showy, scarlet flowers of 'Blaze' are an asset to any red color scheme.

In the red border plan, vines are trained on a fence at the back of the border. Brilliant 'Rouge Cardinal' clematis and trumpet vine share their support with annual flame flower vine and 'Blackie' sweet potato vine, which is admired for its dark bronze summer foliage. If you don't have a fence, the vines may also be wrapped on a pillar or obelisk to provide height in the border.

Roses for the Red Border

Aristocratic 'Geranium' rose, which has a vaselike habit and easily attains a height of 6 or 7 feet (1.8 to 2m), bears bright scarlet flowers for several weeks in late spring, followed by a crop of large, flask-shaped, orange-red hips. This beautiful shrub rose offers a substantial backdrop for perennial companions in the red border.

The scarlet, five-petaled flowers of 'Robusta' rose are truly a knockout. An added bonus: this hardy, upright shrub rose offers its bright flowers in a continuous display from midsummer until frost.

In this plan, the red rambler rose 'Chevy Chase' is trained to grow into a small tree at one end of the border. You can also train it on a fence at the back of the border and grow clematis over it to extend the bloom through the summer. The ever-popular climber 'Blaze' could also be trained over a fence or up a pillar.

Low-growing everblooming roses 'Champlain' and 'Red Ribbons', which bear scarlet-red flowers, complete the plan. The brilliant red flowers of these easy-care roses add their colorful blooms to the mass of perennials, annuals, and accent foliage. Their repeat bloom is a particularly splendid sight, for they provide a focal point of bright color from late spring until hard frost in autumn.

THE RED BORDER
PLANT LIST

1. 'Geranium' rose (*Rosa moyesii* 'Geranium')

2. 'Robusta' rose (*R.* 'Robusta')

3. 'Chevy Chase' rose (*R.* 'Chevy Chase')

4. Trumpet vine (*Campsis* × *tagliabuana* 'Madame Galen')

5. Flame flower vine (*Tropaeolum speciosum*)

6. 'Blackie' sweet potato vine (*Ipomoea batatas* 'Blackie')

7. 'Champlain' rose (*R.* 'Champlain')

8. 'Red Ribbons' (*R.* 'Red Ribbons')

9. Purple smokebush (*Cotinus coggygria* 'Royal Purple')

10. 'Rouge Cardinal' clematis (*Clematis* 'Rouge Cardinal')

11. 'Royal Red' butterfly bush (*Buddleia davidii* 'Royal Red')

12. 'Beauty of Livermore' oriental poppy (*Papaver orientalis* 'Beauty of Livermore') and Chocolate cosmos (*Cosmos atrosanguineus*)

13. 'Chameleon' spurge (*Euphorbia dulcis* 'Chameleon')

14. 'Lucifer' crocosmia (*Crocosmia* 'Lucifer') and 'Little Red Riding Hood' tulip (*Tulipa* 'Little Red Riding Hood')

15. 'Chocolate Ruffles' heuchera (*Heuchera americana* 'Chocolate Ruffles')

16. 'Autumn Red' daylily (*Hemerocallis* 'Autumn Red') and 'Cherry Orchard' tulip (*Tulipa* 'Cherry Orchard')

17. 'Monte Negro' lily (*Lilium* 'Monte Negro')

18. 'Burgundy Giant' purple-leaved fountain grass (*Pennisetum setaceum* 'Burgundy Giant')

19. 'Bishop of Llandaff' dahlia (*Dahlia* 'Bishop of Llandaff') and *Tulipa unicum*

20. 'Strawberry Fields' globe amaranth (*Gomphrena globosa* 'Strawberry Fields')

21. Purple-leaved alternanthera (*Alternanthera dentata* var. *rubrum*)

22. 'Mohawk' canna (*Canna* × *hybrida* 'Mohawk')

23. 'Starry Night' coleus (*Coleus* 'Starry Night')

The Purple Border

This purple border design, which was inspired by the purple border at Sissinghurst Garden in England, favors a range of purple flowers contrasted with dusky reds.

Design Basics

In the purple border the color combinations are subtly rich and striking. 'Atrolineare' Japanese maple provides a lovely focal point with its bronze, cut-leaf foliage. Shrub roses, butterfly bushes, climbing roses, and clematis paint a colorful picture with their flowers in shades of purple highlighted by dusky red roses. Companion perennials such as alliums, striped hollyhocks, geraniums, and asters also add their purple flowers to the mix, which is accented by the red blooms of valerian and knautia. Annuals such as feather celosia and Mexican bush sage carry the bloom to hard frost.

Roses for the Purple Border

The old, richly colored gallica rose 'Charles de Mills' provides deep reddish purple blooms, while the easy-care, compact moss rose 'Nuits de Young' offers velvety, maroon-purple flowers with several layers of petals that contrast beautifully with its gold stamens. Its foliage is also handsome; small green leaves are highlighted with tones of sable brown on dark, prickly stems. Silver-foliage plants complement 'Nuits de Young' best.

'Roseraie de l'Hay', an aristocratic rugosa rose, produces lovely, fragrant, violet-crimson flowers throughout the growing season. Thornless 'Reine des Violettes', which bears scented, grape-colored roses, shares a pillar with deep purple clematis 'Royal Velours' to extend the bloom through summer. Occasionally this Victorian rose also repeats in autumn; deadhead spent flowers in summer to encourage this cherished repeat bloom. In the garden plan shown here, the violet-flowered rambler 'Marie Viaud' is trained on a fence at the back of the border with clematis and other vines.

The roses are underplanted with magenta-red geraniums, violet-purple iris, and salvias, while dwarf striped hollyhocks offer their lavender blooms all summer. Other perennials for the purple border are red valerian, 'Purple Dome' aster, 'Purple Sensation' allium, *Knautia macedonica,* and purple-leaved 'Herrenhausen' marjoram.

Fountain buddleia creates a cascade of lavender flowers in June and 'Black Knight' butterfly bush displays its deep purple spikes well into late summer, when the lovely violet-red rugosa rose 'Roseraie de l'Hay,' is repeating its bloom. Also complementing the rugosa rose is an underplanting of late-summer and autumn perennials, annuals, and tender salvias, which give their best in autumn.

THE PURPLE BORDER
PLANT LIST

1. 'Charles de Mills' rose (*Rosa* 'Charles de Mills')

2. 'Nuits de Young' rose (*R.* 'Nuits de Young')

3. 'Reine des Violettes' rose (*R.* 'Reine des Violettes')

4. 'Roseraie de l'Hay' rose (*R.* 'Roseraie de l'Hay')

5. 'Marie Viaud' rose (*R.* 'Marie Viaud') and Jackman clematis (*Clematis* × *jackmanii*)

6. 'Vyvyan Pennell' clematis (*Clematis* 'Vyvyan Pennell')

7. Hyacinth bean vine (*Dolichos lablab*)

8. 'Atrolineare' Japanese maple (*Acer palmatum* 'Atrolineare')

9. Fountain buddleia (*Buddleia alternifolia*)

10. 'Black Knight' butterfly bush (*Buddleia davidii* 'Black Knight')

11. Dwarf striped hollyhock (*Alcea zebrina*)

12. 'Plumosa' sage (*Salvia nemorosa* 'Plumosa')

13. 'Caesar's Brother' Siberian iris (*Iris sibirica* 'Caesar's Brother')

14. Red valerian (*Centranthus ruber* 'Rosenrot')

15. 'Purple Sensation' allium (*Allium* 'Purple Sensation') and 'Purple Dome' aster (*Aster novae-angliae* 'Purple Dome')

16. 'Herrenhausen' marjoram (*Origanum laevigatum* 'Herrenhausen')

17. Perennial geranium (*Geranium psilostemon*)

18. *Knautia macedonica*

19. 'Purple Feather' celosia (*Celosia spicata* 'Purple Feather')

20. Mexican bush sage (*Salvia leucantha*)

21. 'Purple Rain' sage (*Salvia verticillata* 'Purple Rain')

22. 'Royal Velours' Italian clematis (*Clematis viticella* 'Royal Velours')

The White Border

The white border is given over to creamy white flowers complemented by silver foliage plants. This garden always seems to cool visitors on a hot summer day. A white border is particularly enjoyable at night, when ivory flowers shimmer and glow in the moonlight.

Design Basics

One small specimen tree recommended for the white border is North American native 'Henry Hicks' swamp bay magnolia. This tree is admired for its dark, evergreen foliage that has a silver underleaf, its tough constitution, and its wonderful, fragrant, creamy white summer flowers. If you want to create a dynamite combination in the shade of this small tree, combine 'Love Pat' hostas—boasting crinkled blue foliage and pure white summer flowers—and striking golden-leaved hakone grass. The silver-foliage perennials artemisia, silver thistle, and giant lamb's ear, together with white variegated feather reed grass, provide an interesting foil for the garden's white flowers.

There are also other interesting combinations to try in the white border. Consider planting white-flowered tree peonies, ephemeral old-fashioned bleeding hearts, and pure white autumn anemones for a delightful succession of bloom. Giant kale (*Crambe cordifolia*) contributes the hazy effect of flowers resembling baby's breath, but they are held on huge 5-foot (1.5m) stalks that rise above the roses in early summer. A clump of 'Snowbank' boltonia planted nearby will emerge in summer and provide autumn flowers that are snow white and yellow centered. Lilies and annuals carry the bloom through the summer and in the autumn all of the roses give a glorious encore performance, while 'Honorine Jobert' Japanese anemones chime in with their showy blooms. Low-growing, spreading foreground plants such as white perennial geraniums, creeping *Mazus reptans* 'Alba', and fragrant 'Mrs. Simpkins' dianthus fill the front of the white border with a snowy carpet of blooms. Underplant the perennials with your favorite spring bulbs.

'Blue Mist' fothergilla provides milky bottle-brush flowers in the spring, bluish foliage in the summer, and reddish foliage in autumn. The tree peony 'Godishu' is a great asset to any garden; its huge, single, snowy white flowers enliven the late spring flower border.

❧Roses for the White Border

The snowy white, fragrant climbing tea rose 'Sombreuil' (Zones 6 to 9) is trained against a fence in this white border garden plan, although it can also be grown on a pillar, freestanding tower, or obelisk. Grow 'Venosa Violacea' clematis over the rose for an accent of distinctive small flowers with purple margins that fade to white in the center. The clematis vine will extend bloom on the fence well into summer, and the rose will periodically repeat. You can cover the fence with blooms all season by planting both clematis and long-blooming climbing hydrangea.

In Zones 4 to 5 substitute the hardier alba rose 'Madame Legras de St. Germain' for 'Sombreuil'. Growing 5 to 6 feet (1.5 to 1.8m) tall in a lax habit, 'Madame Legras de St. Germain' is easy to train as a climber, though her nearly thornless canes must be tied to provide support. If space and climate permit, use both 'Sombreuil' and 'Madame Legras de St. Germain' as awe-inspiring climbers.

'Blanc Double de Coubert', a double-flowered, fragrant rugosa rose, is lovely but rambunctious. This rose repels disease and insects and provides abundant spring blooms, repeating through summer. 'Blanc Double de Coubert' looks particularly lovely when paired with pure white foxgloves. Underplant this combination with 'White Swirl' Siberian irises and old-fashioned white bleeding hearts.

If your site has a tree with an open canopy and small leaves that allow light to penetrate (such as crab apple or cherry), use it as a support for the snowy white, fragrant scrambler 'Seagull', which is also perfect for covering a fence at the back of the border. Other white-flowered roses include the enchanting, everblooming classic rose 'Gruss an Aachen', with its clusters of carmine-tinted buds that open to double, fragrant, blush-tinted blooms which age to creamy white. 'Sea Foam' and 'Jeepers Creepers', which are both admirable, easy-care groundcover roses, complete the rose selection for the white border design.

TOP: *'Gruss an Aachen'*
❀
ABOVE: *'Sombreuil'*
❀

135

THE WHITE BORDER

PLANT LIST

1. 'Blanc Double de Coubert' rose (*Rosa* 'Blanc Double de Coubert')

2. 'Gruss an Aachen' rose (*R.* 'Gruss an Aachen')

3. 'Sea Foam' rose (*R.* 'Seafoam')

4. 'Jeepers Creepers' rose (*R.* 'Jeepers Creepers')

5. 'Sombreuil' climbing tea rose (*R.* 'Sombreuil'); if desired, intertwine with 'Venosa Violacea' Italian clematis (*Clematis viticella* 'Venosa Violacea')

6. 'Seagull' rose (*R.* 'Seagull')

7. *Clematis lanuginosa candida*

8. Climbing hydrangea (*Hydrangea anomala petiolaris*)

9. 'Henry Hicks' swamp bay magnolia (*Magnolia virginiana* 'Henry Hicks')

10. 'Blue Mist' fothergilla (*Fothergilla gardenii* 'Blue Mist')

11. Silver thistle (*Onopordum acanthium*)

12. 'Godishu' tree peony (*Paeonia suffruticosa* 'Godishu')

13. White foxglove (*Digitalis purpurea* 'Alba'); if desired, interplant 'Sonata' cosmos (*Cosmos bipinnatus* 'Sonata')

14. Siberian iris (*Iris sibirica* 'White Swirl')

15. Giant kale (*Crambe cordifolia*) and boltonia (*Boltonia asteroides* 'Snowdrift')

16. White old-fashioned bleeding heart (*Dicentra spectabilis* 'Alba'); if desired, interplant 'Honorine Jobert' anemone (*Anemone* × *hybrida* 'Honorine Jobert')

17. 'Mrs. Simpkins' pinks (*Dianthus* 'Mrs. Simpkins')

18. 'Casablanca' lily (*Lilium* 'Casablanca')

19. *Mazus reptans* 'Alba'

20. White perennial geranium (*Geranium sanquineum* var. *album*)

21. 'Love Pat' hosta (*Hosta* 'Love Pat'); if desired, also plant wood hyacinth (*Scilla campanulata*)

22. Hakone grass (*Hakonechloa macra* 'Aureola')

23. 'Huntington Gardens' artemisia (*Artemisia* 'Huntington Gardens')

24. Purple ghost plant (*Artemisia lactiflora* 'Guihzo')

25. Giant lamb's ears (*Stachys* 'Helene von Stein')

26. 'Overdam' feather reed grass (*Calamagrostis acutiflora* 'Overdam')

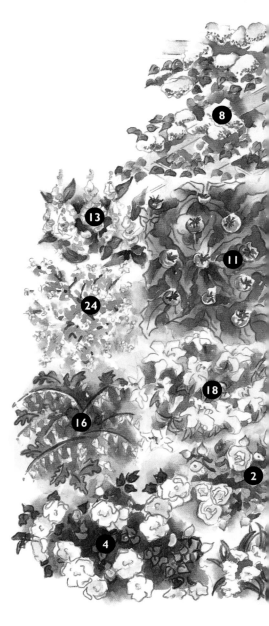

ABOVE, FROM LEFT TO RIGHT: Rosa rugosa, '*City of York*', '*Dortmund*'.
❀

SEASIDE GARDEN:
Salt-Tolerant Roses, Shrubs, Ornamental Grasses, and Flowers

The seaside garden is brimming with roses, other flowers, and ornamental grasses that thrive in the salt air, sandy soil, and hot sunshine associated with coastal areas. Sandy soil tends to be so well drained that it often becomes droughty, and recommended plants such as rugosa rose (also known as sea tomato), bayberry, sea kale, and rock rose are well adapted to harsh, seaside conditions. The seaside garden is particularly colorful from late May through early autumn, when many of the plants offer late-season interest with their attractive seedheads, fruits, and autumn blooms.

❀Design Basics

In the seaside garden plan red rugosa rose (*Rosa rugosa* var. *rubra*) is planted as a hedge, and the climbing roses adorn a fence. Memorial rose covers a raised bed near the patio in the backyard and a simple mixed border along the back fence completes the plan. Good shrubs for seaside plantings include hydrangea, sweet pepper bush, low bush blueberry, potentilla, and 'Hansa' rose; these shrubs give some substance to the planting, which is enhanced by the flowers of Russian sage, rock rose, sea kale, and sedum.

Roses for the Seaside Garden

The best roses for the seaside garden not only tolerate the salt air and dry, sunny conditions, but thrive in this inhospitable environment. The rugosa rose makes its home in the sand dunes; its single, fragrant flowers bloom continuously throughout the growing season and are followed by cherry-tomatolike hips in late summer. *Rosa rugosa* var. *rubra* produces single, violet-red flowers all summer, and in late summer and autumn it bears lovely hips. Purple, scented flowers on a tall, vase-shaped shrub are the sterling qualities of aristocratic 'Hansa'. 'Hansa' can be underplanted with black mondo grass and 'Bowles' Golden' sedge.

Don't exclude roses from your garden just because you live with salt air and sandy soil. There are many roses available that will flourish in the difficult conditions of a seaside garden.

Memorial rose (*Rosa wichuraiana*) is another coastal rose that can be used as a groundcover. Studded with fragrant, single white flowers that are attractively displayed all summer against polished dark green foliage, memorial rose is also parent to a host of tough, care-free climbers that are a familiar sight in seaside gardens. On Nantucket, for instance, popular wichuraiana climbers such as 'American Pillar' and 'Dr. W. Van Fleet' were frequently used to blanket cottages with their cascading blooms. Many of the great old wichuraiana climbers are simply indestructible and they still grow and thrive on the seaside cottages, though they were planted nearly a century ago.

In this seaside garden plan, several excellent climbers with memorial rose ancestry are used as fence-huggers. 'City of York' is one of the best white care-free climbers; its scented semidouble flowers are pure white and are produced in large clusters in early summer. If you deadhead the spent flowers, this rose will give a few late-summer flowers as well.

'Dortmund' inherits its free-blooming, disease-resistant nature from its ancestors *R. rugosa* and *R. wichuraiana*. It features huge clusters of large, five-petaled, red flowers branded with a white eye. This eye-catching rose is a knockout in full bloom, and offers repeat bloom if it is religiously deadheaded.

THE SEASIDE GARDEN
PLANT LIST

1. Memorial rose (*Rosa wichuraiana*)

2. 'City of York' rose (*R.* 'City of York')

3. 'Dortmund' rose (*R.* 'Dortmund')

4. Red rugosa rose (*R. rugosa* var. *rubra*)

5. 'Hansa' rose (*R.* 'Hansa')

6. 'Toyko Delight' hydrangea (*Hydrangea* 'Tokyo Delight')

7. Phlomis (*Phlomis fruticosa*)

8. Dwarf blueberry (*Vaccinium vitis-idaea*)

9. 'Yellow Queen' potentilla (*Potentilla hybrida* 'Yellow Queen')

10. 'Vera Jameson' sedum (*Sedum* × 'Vera Jameson')

11. 'Wisley Primrose' rock rose (*Helianthemum nummularium* 'Wisley Primrose')

12. Sea kale (*Crambe maritima*)

13. Perennial geranium (*Geranium cinereum* 'Ballerina')

14. 'Pewter Veil' heuchera (*Heuchera americana* 'Pewter Veil')

15. Red switchgrass (*Panicum virgatum* 'Hanse Hermes')

16. Russian sage (*Perovskia atriplicifolia*)

17. Bayberry (*Myrica pensylvanica*)

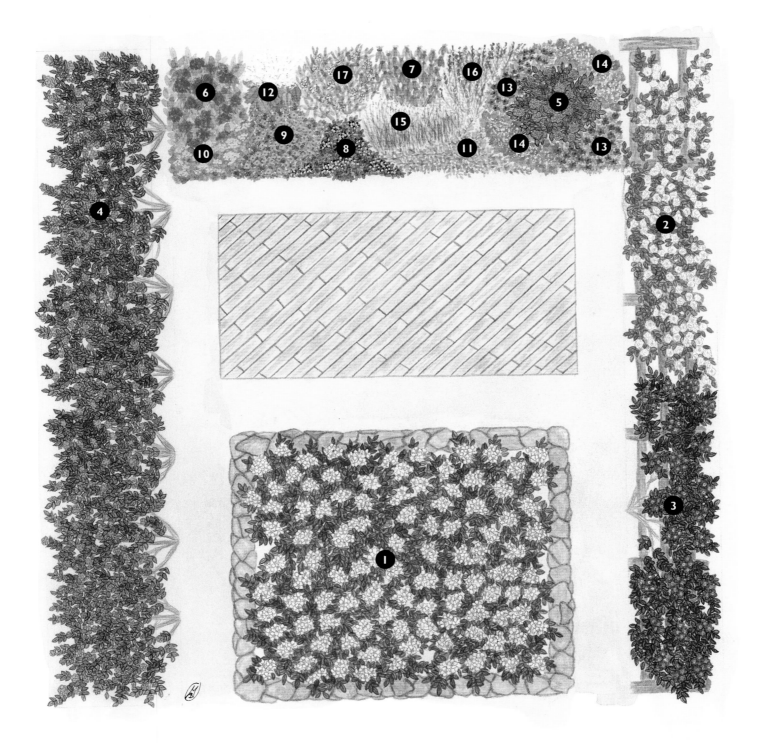

FORMAL ENTRANCE GARDEN AND ROSE WALK:
A Rose and Boxwood Classic

Provide a dramatic passage to your door or garden with a formal entrance garden and rose walk. Two versions of a rose walk are shown in these simple, elegant designs; each employs roses, lavender or catmint, and small-leaved boxwood.

❧ Design Basics

In the first plan, 'The Fairy' weeping standard roses are underplanted with lavender and edged with box. The rose's clear pink pompon-shaped flowers are attractively complemented by the lavender's blue flowers and silver foliage. 'The Fairy' is the best choice for a weeping standard because it possesses a graceful habit, extreme adaptability, and excellent disease resistance, and is readily available to gardeners.

The second plan uses a simple rose hedge to define the formal entrance garden. The best choice is a tough, disease-free shrub that can be neatly clipped, such as 'Frau Dagmar Hartopp' rose. This compact rugosa hybrid bears large, five-petaled, silver-pink blooms nonstop, produces hips as large as cherry tomatoes in late summer, and offers golden-bronze foliage in autumn. This rose is easy to maintain as a hedge and looks beautiful underplanted with blue spikes of garden catmint. For tall blue spires later in the season, substitute Russian sage for the catmint. The box edging gives a crisp evergreen effect for winter beauty. These simple, colorful displays provide all-season interest and beautifully embellish the entrance to your house or garden.

❧ Roses for the Rose Walk

Roses for hedging and formal walks should be easy to care for and disease-resistant, and they should also possess excellent ornamental characteristics such as repeat bloom and handsome, glossy foliage. The best and most versatile of the polyantha or sweetheart roses, 'The Fairy' is an international favorite. Used as a weeping standard to edge a walk, it provides both nonstop flowers and an interesting tree-rose formality. Its clear pink flower clusters always look great in combination with blooms in shades of blue.

'Frau Dagmar Hartopp' makes a fine hedge and is decidedly the best overall performer and most useful of the compact hybrid rugosa roses. Large, fragrant, silver-pink flowers, beautiful, glossy foliage, and bright red hips make this rose an all-season charmer. For a larger hedge in pure white, try *Rosa rugosa* var. *alba*. Other excellent hedging roses in violet-red are *Rosa rugosa* var. *rubra* and 'Dart's Dash'.

Roses make elegant additions to formal gardens of every description, and are particularly pleasing in an entrance garden, where they can be enjoyed as you come and go throughout the day.

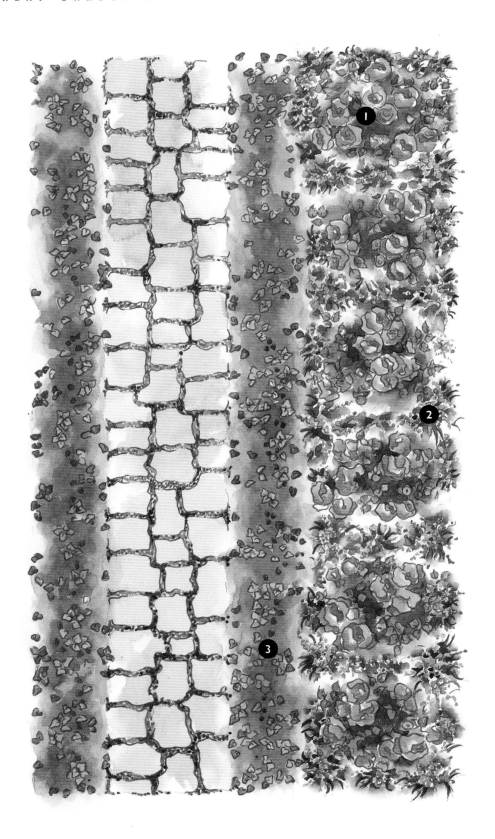

FORMAL ENTRANCE GARDEN

PLANT LIST 1

1. 'The Fairy' rose (*Rosa* 'The Fairy')

2. 'Provence' lavender *(Lavandula* × *intermedia* 'Provence')

3. 'Green Gem' hybrid boxwood (*Buxus* hybrid 'Green Gem')

FORMAL ENTRANCE GARDEN

PLANT LIST II

1. 'Frau Dagmar Hartopp' rose (*Rosa* 'Frau Dagmar Hartopp')

2. 'Dropmore' garden catmint (*Nepeta* × *faassenii* 'Dropmore')

3. 'Green Mound' hybrid boxwood (*Buxus* hybrid 'Green Mound')

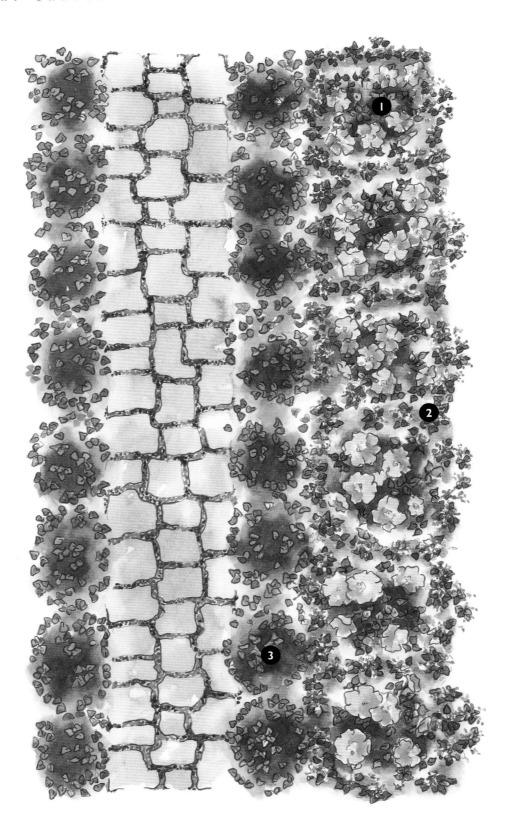

CHILDREN'S GARDEN:
Miniature Roses Mixed with Fuzzy, Bright, and Scented Plants

The children's garden is a special place that gives kids a chance to get to know plants: to tend, touch, pick, and smell them. It is full of colorful perennial and annual flowers both giant- and baby-size; tiny roses; soft, fuzzy leaves; and wonderful fragrance. Kids can stick their fingers in the snapdragon's mouth, pet the lamb's ears, eat the nasturtiums, smell the marigolds, finger the pipe-cleanerlike flowers of Mexican sage, and pick a bouquet of thimble-size roses. Children are also intrigued by winged visitors such as hummingbirds and butterflies, which can easily be attracted to the garden. Best of all, this garden is designed especially for kids, and gives them a great place to cool off or hide out in the vine-covered tepee.

Design Basics

This plan shows a sunny raised bed divided by crossing flagstone paths for easy access. In the center of the garden, a vine-covered tepee provides a shady respite. The tepee is easily constructed using 10-foot (3m) wooden poles. Cover the tepee frame with wire or plastic mesh, which provides a webbed surface perfect for supporting clinging vines; around the base of the poles, plant colorful annual and perennial vines to cover the tepee. Fast-growing annual morning glory, black-eyed Susan vine, and firecracker vine will all provide quick cover, while perennial trumpet honeysuckle and clematis gradually twine up the poles and cover the structure. Be sure to leave an opening that can be used for an entrance. Use a gravel mulch in the tepee bed and remember to include a few large and small rocks to delight the kids.

In four small beds flanking the tepee you can include a variety of plants attractive to children. Annuals play an important part in this garden, and kids can learn how to start them from seed indoors or sow them directly in the garden beds. Many flowers and vegetables are easy to grow from seed. A few rows of corn are sure to appeal to kids, as do giant sunflowers, cherry tomatoes, marigolds, and snapdragons. Annuals can easily be rotated so that from year to year the kids learn to appreciate

OPPOSITE: The tiny blooms of miniature roses fascinate old and young alike. These bright yellow roses add a sunny aspect to a small bed encircling a birdbath.

147

growing their old favorites as well as untried varieties of flowers, vegetables, and even fruits.

Be sure to leave plenty of room in the four beds for kids to move about. Plant vegetables and strawberries in rows for easy access and mulch the paths. Including a series of stepping stones in the flower gardens makes getting around as fun and easy for kids as a game of hopscotch.

Roses for the Children's Garden

The best roses for kids are the miniatures, which give thimble-size blooms from early summer through frost with minimal care. 'Teddy Bear', 'Cinderella', 'Little Mermaid', 'Baby Katy', 'Little Artist', 'Cupcake', and 'Magic Carrousel' are just a few of the many tiny roses in a rainbow of colors that kids can learn to grow and enjoy. Miniatures are among the easiest and most satisfying of all roses to grow, and are perfect for a sunny spot in a children's garden. A warning to parents: miniature roses are complete with tiny thorns, so encourage children to be careful and to wear gardening gloves when working with any roses.

If larger rose flowers appeal to you and your child, you can substitute a few of these for the miniatures in the plan. You might wish to choose the most disease-resistant and trouble-free roses—such as 'Carefree Wonder' or 'Carefree Beauty'—so your child won't face the disappointment of failing roses.

Fruits for the Children's Garden

The children's garden is a perfect place to try bright, easy-to-grow fruits. Strawberries are a great choice because even a small patch yields lots of fruit in the first few years. When the strawberry plants begin to decline, replant them or try another small fruit. Raspberries and blackberries are also appealing, delicious, and easy to grow, but remember that their canes are very prickly (and therefore unsuitable for very young children) and they sucker freely and need to be confined to a particular patch so that they don't overrun the garden.

☙Attracting Wildlife to the Children's Garden

Children are fascinated by hummingbirds, bees, butterflies, and other insects that visit flowers. If you plant morning glories and honeysuckle to cover the tepee, then hummingbirds will visit your garden. However, you can also tailor your annuals to include those attractive to hummingbirds. These delicate little birds are lured by tubular flowers, so try larkspurs, cleome, canna, petunias, nasturtiums, sweet Williams, nicotiana, shrub verbena, hollyhocks, and salvias.

Butterflies are particularly easy to attract and they really do visit the plants that carry their name, especially butterfly bush and butterfly weed. Butterflies and butterfly bushes are well loved by adults and children alike, and many of the garden designs in this book incorporate this lovely, fragrant, summer-blooming shrub, which produces elegant flower spires in shades from pure white to deep purple.

CHILDREN'S GARDEN

PLANT LIST

1. 'Teddy Bear' rose (*Rosa* 'Teddy Bear')

2. 'Cinderella' rose (*R.* 'Cinderella')

3. 'Little Mermaid' rose (*R.* 'Little Mermaid')

4. 'Little Artist' rose (*R.* 'Little Artist')

5. 'Cupcake' rose (*R.* 'Cupcake')

6. *Clematis montana*

7. Sweet autumn clematis (*Clematis maximowicziana*)

8. Trumpet honeysuckle (*Lonicera sempervirens*)

9. 'Chocolate' morning glory (*Ipomoea imperialis* 'Chocolate')

10. Firecracker vine (*Mina lobata* 'Exotic Love')

11. Butterfly bush (*Buddleia davidii* 'Nanho Purple')

12. 'Stella d'Oro' daylily (*Hemerocallis* 'Stella d'Oro')

13. Giant lamb's ears (*Stachys* 'Helene von Stein')

14. Giant allium (*Allium giganteum*) and purple coneflower (*Echinacea purpurea* 'Magnus')

15. 'Coronation Gold' yarrow (*Achillea* × 'Coronation Gold')

16. 'Disco Belle' hibiscus (*Hibiscus moscheutos* 'Disco Belle')

17. 'Lime Green' nicotiana (*Nicotiana alata* 'Lime Green')

18. 'Cherry Queen' spider plant (*Cleome spinosa* 'Cherry Queen')

19. 'Tropical Rose' canna (*Canna indica* 'Tropical Rose')

20. 'Madness Plum Crazy' petunia (*Petunia* 'Madness Plum Crazy')

21. 'Tom Thumb Mixed' nasturtium (*Tropaeolum nanum* 'Tom Thumb Mixed')

22. Mexican sage (*Salvia leucantha*)

23. 'Ozark Beauty' strawberry (*Fragaria* × *ananassa* 'Ozark Beauty')

24. 'Sunspot' sunflower (*Helianthus annuus* 'Sunspot')

25. 'Silver Choice' corn (*Zea mays* var. *rugosa* 'Silver Choice')

26. 'Cinderella Mixed' snapdragon (*Antirrhinum majus* 'Cinderella Mix')

27. 'Gardener's Delight' cherry tomato (*Lycopersicon lycopersicum* 'Gardener's Delight')

28. Butterfly weed (*Asclepias curassavica*)

29. 'Jaguar' French marigold (*Tagetes tenuifolia* 'Jaguar')

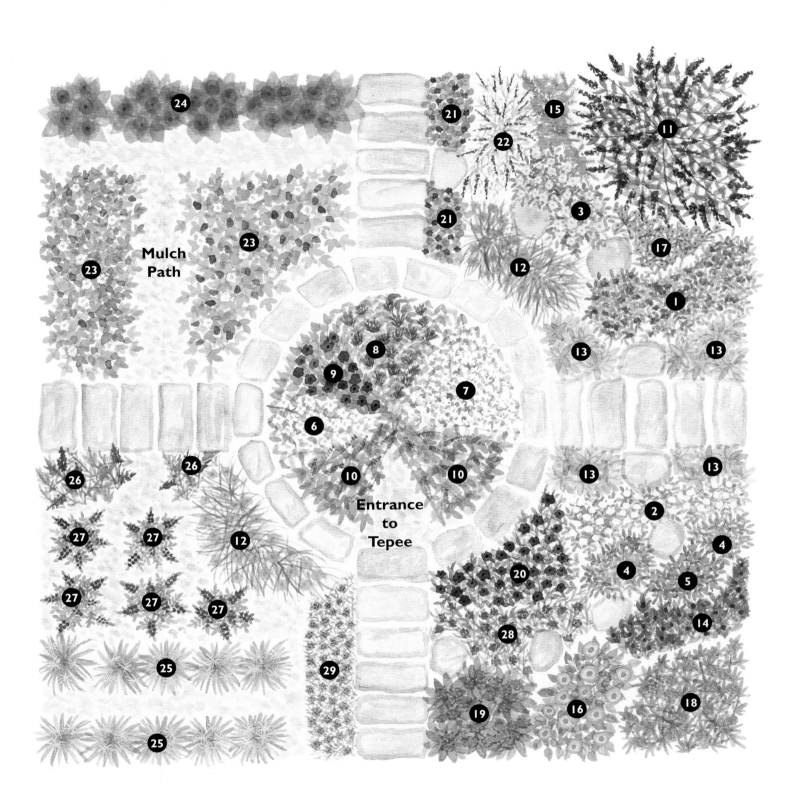

Mulch
Path

Entrance
to
Tepee

BIRD AND BUTTERFLY GARDEN:
A Wild Garden Filled with Meadow Flowers and Grasses

Even in a small space you can grow plants that bear flowers and fruits attractive to butterflies and birds. Many North American meadow plants—including sunflowers, daisies, butterfly weed, and asters—are in the business of attracting butterflies and hummingbirds, which pollinate their flowers. Likewise, trees and shrubs that bear small fruits are magnets for birds; roses and rose family members such as blackberries, hawthorn, and crab apple as well as virbunums and hollies attract birds with their brightly colored fruits, and their seeds are then spread far and wide. Growing any of these plants, along with a host of others, will ensure visits from butterflies and birds. The backyard meadow garden design shown here is also alive with the movement of ornamental grasses swaying in the wind, and many of the plants in the plan will beautify your yard year-round with flowers, fruit, brilliantly colored autumn foliage, and persistent seeds and berries that attract resident birds in winter.

Rugosa rose and other wild roses produce an abundance of fruits attractive to birds.

🌼 Design Basics

Overflowing with plants attractive to birds and butterflies, this wild garden suggests a meadow in its simple combinations. Enjoy a meadow scene—waving grasses, flowers, seedheads, and winter fruits—complete with wildlife year-round in your own backyard. Don't forget to allow for some chance self-sowing of these meadow plants, which will subtly change the garden year by year. The centerpiece for this garden is the kousa dogwood, which provides interest through all the seasons with its flowers, fruits, autumn foliage color, and peeling bark, displayed best in winter when the leaves have fallen.

🌼 Roses for the Bird and Butterfly Garden

Birds visit roses that produce fruit, or rose hips, on which they can feed in autumn and winter. Wild roses are the most reliable hip-bearing types. White rugosa rose (*Rosa rugosa* var. *alba*) is a handsome, tough shrub; its fragrant, exquisite single flowers are generously produced in late spring through late summer and are followed by large, cherry tomato–size hips. Helen rose

152

(*R. helenae*) is usually grown as a rambler and is covered in clusters of small white flowers in early summer, with hips ripening in late summer. Some of the North American species roses are great draws for birds and provide excellent autumn foliage color. Prairie rose (*R. setigera*), for one, is a good hip producer and its lax habit makes it suitable as a mounding groundcover; covered with single pink blooms in early summer, this rose's autumn foliage is scarlet. Virginia rose (*R. virginiana*) forms an upright suckering shrub studded with pink single flowers in early summer; hips ripen on the red stems in late summer and persist through winter. Autumn foliage color is orange-red.

Roses are a natural choice for a wild garden; thorny canes offer a protected place for birds to perch while feeding on autumn hips.

❧ Shrubs and Trees Attractive to Birds

Winterberry holly attracts birds to the winter garden and offers its brilliant, jewellike scarlet berries well into February. Kousa dogwood—one of the most handsome small, flowering specimen trees—produces round, dusky red, fleshy, late-summer fruits that are favored by birds. Blueberries delight us, but if you plant highbush blueberry its tasty fruits will also bring birds to the garden in midsummer. Hummingbirds are particularly attracted to tubular flowers, including those produced by 'Hummingbird' sweet pepper bush and rose of Sharon.

❧ Flowers Attractive to Butterflies

The lavender flower spikes, silver leaves, and compact habit of 'Lochnich' butterfly bush make it one of the best of the buddleia group. Monarch butterflies look beautiful gathering nectar from its lavender flowers dotted with an orange eye. Flowers of bluebeard, hosta, coreopsis, butterfly weed, purple coneflower, goldenrod, shrub verbena, and false sunflower also attract butterflies to the garden. Planting the flowers in drifts maximizes their impact as butterfly-attractors.

BIRD AND BUTTERFLY GARDEN

PLANT LIST

1. White rugose rose (*Rosa rugosa* var. *alba*)

2. Helen rose (*R. helenae*)

3. Prairie rose (*R. setigera*) or Virginia rose (*R. virginiana*)

4. Kousa dogwood (*Cornus kousa*)

5. Winterberry holly (*Ilex verticillata* 'Winter Red')

6. Highbush blueberry (*Vaccinium coryumbosum*)

7. Sweet pepper bush (*Clethra alnifolia* 'Hummingbird')

8. 'Lochnich' butterfly bush (*Buddleia* × 'Lochnich')

9. 'Dark Knight' bluebeard (*Caryopteris* × *clandonensis* 'Dark Knight')

10. Compact abelia (*Abelia* × *grandiflora* 'Francis Mason')

11. Blue switchgrass (*Panicum virgatum* 'Heavy Metal')

12. Japanese silver grass (*Miscanthus sinensis* 'Morning Light')

13. Little bluestem (*Schizachyrium scoparium*)

14. 'Joan Senior' daylily (*Hemerocallis* 'Joan Senior')

15. 'Gardenview Scarlet' bee balm (*Monarda didyma* 'Gardenview Scarlet')

16. 'Fireland' yarrow (*Achillea millefolium* 'Fireland')

17. 'Moonbeam' coreopsis (*Coreopsis verticillata* 'Moonbeam')

18. 'Gay Butterflies' butterfly weed (*Asclepias tuberosa* 'Gay Butterflies')

19. 'Karat' false sunflower (*Heliopsis helianthoides* 'Karat')

20. 'Fireworks' goldenrod (*Solidago rugosa* 'Fireworks')

21. 'Kabitan' hosta (*Hosta* 'Kabitan')

22. 'Bowles Golden' sedge (*Carex elata* 'Bowles Golden')

23. Lantana (*Lantana camara*)

24. Japanese aster (*Kalimeris integrifolia*)

25. 'Blue Hill' sage (*Salvia nemorosa* 'Blue Hill')

26. Tall verbena (*Verbena bonariensis*)

27. Christmas rose (*Helleborus niger*) and Lenten rose (*H. orientalis*)

28. 'Ego' Siberian iris (*Iris sibirica* 'Ego')

29. Bluestar (*Amsonia hubrechtii*)

30. 'Gateway' Joe Pye weed (*Eupatorium maculatum* 'Gateway')

31. 'Karl Foerster' feather reed grass (*Calamagrostis acutiflora* 'Karl Foerster')

32. 'Magnus' purple coneflower (*Echinacea purpurea* 'Magnus')

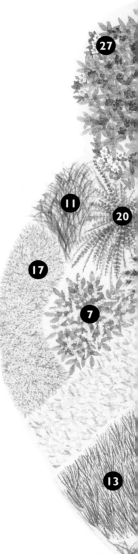

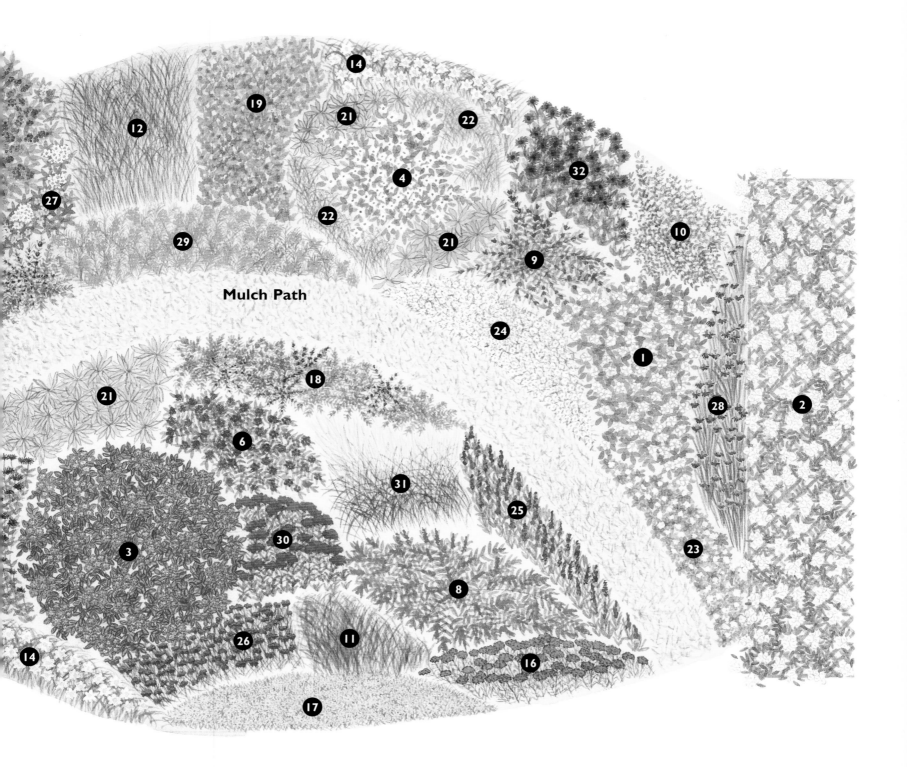

Mulch Path

PLANT HARDINESS ZONES

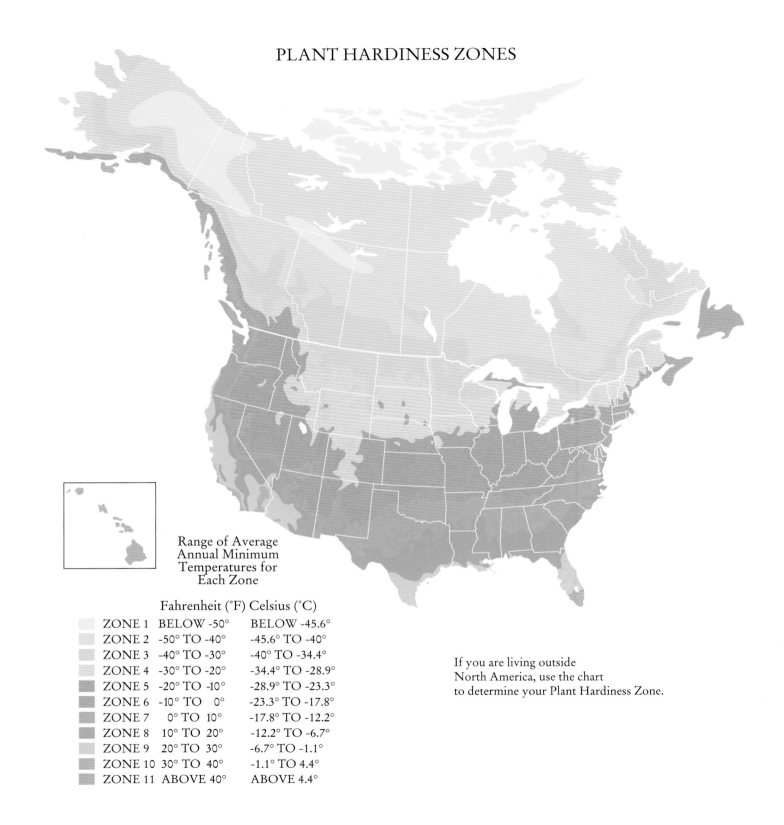

Range of Average
Annual Minimum
Temperatures for
Each Zone

		Fahrenheit (°F)	Celsius (°C)
	ZONE 1	BELOW -50°	BELOW -45.6°
	ZONE 2	-50° TO -40°	-45.6° TO -40°
	ZONE 3	-40° TO -30°	-40° TO -34.4°
	ZONE 4	-30° TO -20°	-34.4° TO -28.9°
	ZONE 5	-20° TO -10°	-28.9° TO -23.3°
	ZONE 6	-10° TO 0°	-23.3° TO -17.8°
	ZONE 7	0° TO 10°	-17.8° TO -12.2°
	ZONE 8	10° TO 20°	-12.2° TO -6.7°
	ZONE 9	20° TO 30°	-6.7° TO -1.1°
	ZONE 10	30° TO 40°	-1.1° TO 4.4°
	ZONE 11	ABOVE 40°	ABOVE 4.4°

If you are living outside
North America, use the chart
to determine your Plant Hardiness Zone.

Glossary

Bareroot bush A dormant bush without soil around its roots. Bareroot bushes are easily handled, and so plants are commonly shipped this way. Mail-order suppliers will ship bareroot bushes at the appropriate time for planting in your region.

Blackspot Fungal disease that causes rose leaves to spot, turn yellow, and drop from the bush.

Cultivar A horticultural variety that results from selective hybridization or arises from a sport (see **Sport**).

Deadhead The practice of pruning off spent flowers, which encourages repeat bloom.

Double A flower that has more than twenty petals.

Espalier A plant trained to grow in one plane on a wall, lattice, or trellis.

Herbaceous A nonwoody plant.

Humus Organic matter; decaying animal or vegetable matter such as compost or manure. Humus is an important component of good garden soil.

Hybrid A plant resulting from a cross between two or more parents.

Layering Simple asexual method of propagation in which a cane is bent down and partly covered with soil so that it will form roots.

Modern rose Any rose or rose class introduced since 1867, the year the hybrid tea was introduced.

Old garden rose Any rose or rose class, including species roses, in existence before 1867.

Propagation Reproducing plants using sexual or asexual methods. Sexual production is from seed and results in offspring different from parents; asexual production (cloning) results in offspring identical to its parent. Asexual production techniques include propagation by cuttings layering, grafting, budding, and tissue culture.

Semidouble A flower that has eight to twenty petals.

Single A flower that has five to eight petals.

Sport A genetic mutation; usually a shoot from a single bud different in some way from the variety that produced it. A famous example is 'New Dawn' climbing rose, which arose as a sport from the climber 'Dr. W. Van Fleet'.

Standard A "tree" rose; a rose variety grafted onto an interstem 2 to 4 feet (0.6 to 1.2m) tall so that it simulates a slender tree form.

Sweetheart rose Synonym for a polyantha rose; a repeat-blooming dwarf shrub that produces sprays of many small flowers, such as 'Cecile Brunner' and 'The Fairy'.

Resources

United States

Antique Rose Emporium
Rt. 5, Box 143
Brenham, TX 77833
Own-root, bareroot, and container roses

The Roseraie at Bayfields
PO Box R
Waldoboro, ME 04572
Hardy roses

Carroll Gardens
444 East Main Street
PO Box 310
Westminster, MD 21158
Modern and antique roses

Edmunds' Roses
6235 SW Kahle Road
Wilsonville, OR 97070
Hybrid tea roses

Forevergreen Farm
Royall River Roses
70 New Gloucester Road
North Yarmouth, ME 04097
Hardy roses

Greenmantle Nursery
3010 Ettersburg Road
Garberville, CA 95542
Own-root heritage roses

Heirloom Old Garden Roses
24062 Riverside Drive NE
St. Paul, OR 97137
Own-root and container roses

Heritage Rose Gardens, Rosequus
40350 Wilderness Road
Branscomb, CA 95417
Own-root roses

High Country Rosarium
1717 Downing Street
Denver, CO 80218
Minimum order: 10 plants
Own-root old garden roses

Historical Roses
1657 West Jackson Street
Painesville, OH 44077

Jackson & Perkins
One Rose Lane
Medford, OR 97501-0702

Modern roses
Justice Miniature Roses
5947 SW Kahle Road
Wilsonville, OR 97070

Lowe's Own Root Roses
6 Sheffield Road
Nashua, NH 03062
Own-root heritage roses

Moore Miniature Roses
Sequoia Nursery
2519 East Noble Avenue
Visalia, CA 93277

Nor'East Miniature Roses, Inc.
PO Box 307
Rowley, MA 01969

Oregon Miniature Roses, Inc.
8285 SW 185th Avenue
Beaverton, OR 97007-5742

The Rose Ranch
PO Box 10087
Salinas, CA 93912
Own-root old and rare roses

Roses of Yesterday and Today
802 Brown's Valley Road
Watsonville, CA 95076

York Hill Farm
271 N. Haverhill Road
Kensington, NH 03833
Heritage roses

Australia

Cox's Nursery
RMB 216 Oaks Road
Thirlmere NSW 2572

Ross Roses
St. Andrew's Terrace
Willunga SA 5172

S. Brundrett & Sons (Roses) Pty Ltd
Brundrett Road
Narre Warren North VIC 3804

Treloar Roses
Midwood
Portland VIC 3305

Canada

Corn Hill Nursery, Ltd.
RR 5
Petitcodiac, NB E0A 2H0
Hardy roses; own-root roses

Hortico, Inc.
723 Robson Road
RR 1
Waterdown, Ontario L0R 2H1
Hardy and old roses

Pickering Nurseries, Inc.
670 Kingston Road
Pickering, Ontario L1V 1A6
Antique and rare roses

Europe

Peter Beales Roses
London Road
Attleborough, Norfolk, NR17 1AY
England
Old garden roses

Cants of Colchester, Ltd.
Nayland Road, Mile End
Colchester, Essex CO4 5EB
England

Georges Delbard SA
16 Quai de la Megisserie
75038 Paris Cedex 01
France

W. Kordes Söhne
Rosenstrabe 54
Offenseth-Sparrieshoop, Germany
Minimum order: 10 plants

Organizations

The American Rose Society
PO Box 30,000
Shreveport, LA 71130

The Canadian Rose Society
10 Fairfax Crescent
Scarborough, Ontario M1L 1Z8

The Royal National Rose Society
Chiswell Green
St. Albans, Hertfordshire AL2 3NR
England

Photography Credits

Front jacket photography: ©R. Todd Davis: center; ©Dency Kane: corners

Back Jacket Photography: ©John Glover: bottom left; ©Jerry Pavia: top right; ©Clive Nichols: background

©David Coppin: pp. 1, 16, 31, 32 center, 32 bottom, 34, 81 bottom
©R. Todd Davis: pp. 29, 111 right, 127, 146, 153
©Ken Druse: pp. 60, 86 right, 107, 139
©John Glover: pp. endpapers, 6 top, 10 (Designer: David Stevens), 10, 18, 19 top, 23, 42, 50, 55, 56, 73, 81 top, 92, 93, 94, 103 top, 103 bottom, 111 left
©Dency Kane: pp. 6 center, 7, 11 right, 13, 15, 24, 27, 32 top, 36, 37, 38, 40, 41, 43, 45, 48-49, 57 bottom, 64 center, 68, 75, 77 center, 77 bottom, 87, 105, 106, 111 center, 114, 126, 135 top, 135 bottom, 138 left, 138 right
©Judith C. McKeon: p. 86 center
©Allan Mandell: pp. 28, 53, 74, 80, 115
©Charles Mann: pp. 30, 59, 143
©Rick Mark: p. 17
©Clive Nichols: pp. 2 (Designer: Claus Scheinert), 9 (Designer: A. Lennox-Boyd), 14, 20, 25, 58, 62, 72, 79, 83, 90, 101, 102, 104, 118, 121, 124, 130 bottom, 131
©Jerry Pavia: pp. 46, 61, 63, 69, 82, 96, 97, 148 bottom, 149
PHOTO/NATS, INC.: ©Priscilla Connell: p. 120; ©John A. Lynch: p. 11 center; ©Sydney Karp: p. 152; ©Ann Reilly: pp. 5, 6 bottom, 11 left, 12, 57 top, 64 right, 67, 70, 77 top, 78, 86 left, 110, 119, 130 top, 138 center, 148 top ; ©Albert Squillace: pp. 8, 19 bottom, 76; ©Virginia Twinam-Smith: pp. 26, 35; ©Barbara Woike: p. 64 left
VISUALS UNLIMITED: ©Dick Keen: p. 66

Illustration
Jennifer S. Markson: pp. 85, 89, 99, 116-117, 122-123, 141, 151, 154-155

Susan B. Kemnitz: pp. 91, 109, 113, 128-129, 132-133, 136-137, 144, 145

Index